BEGINNER'S
Welsh

WITH 2 AUDIO CDs

Hippocrene Beginner's Series

Also Available

HIPPOCRENE BEGINNER'S SERIES

BEGINNER'S
Welsh
WITH 2 AUDIO CDs

Heini Gruffudd

HIPPOCRENE BOOKS, INC.
New York

1ˢᵗ paperback-with-audio edition 2008

ISBN of previous edition: 0-7818-0589-9

For information, address:
   Hippocrene Books, Inc.
   171 Madison Avenue
   New York, NY 10016
   www.hippocrenebooks.com

Library of Congress Cataloging-in-Publication Data

Gruffudd, Heini.
   Beginner's Welsh : with 2 audio CDs / Heini Gruffudd.—1st pbk.-with-audio ed.
   p.   cm.
   ISBN-13: 978-0-7818-1160-6 (pbk.)
   ISBN-10: 0-7818-1160-0 (pbk.)
      1. Welsh language—Textbooks for foreign speakers—English. 2. Welsh
   language—Grammar—Problems, exercises, etc. I. Title.

PB2123.G74 2007
491.6'682421—dc22   2007017781

Printed in the United States of America.

I'm hwyresau a'm hŵyr,
Gwenllian, Greta a Dafydd Sion

Ennill llwyr yw ennill iaith

Diolch i'r Americaniaid dros dro canlynol am
gymorth gyda'r CD:
Catrin Brace, Guto Harri, Carys Jones, Gwenfair Vaughan
Jones a Philip Davies

Contents

Introduction

The Welsh language and its rich culture and heritage have survived successfully into the twenty-first century, in spite of having
to compete with its large neighbor, English. As of the 2001 census,
more than 659,000 people speak Welsh, approximately 23 percent
of the total population of nearly three million, and they are spread
fairly equally numerically throughout the country. By proportion of
Welsh speakers, the western and northern parts of Wales are more
Welsh-speaking.

Many people come to Britain not knowing that Wales exists, or
that a different language has been spoken here for sixteen hundred
years. Fewer still realize that Welsh, or old Welsh, and its ancestor,
Brythoneg, or 'Britannic', was the language spoken over most of the
territory of Britain before the English had thought of coming here.
Today, Welsh as a spoken language is more or less limited to Wales,
but there are communities of Welsh speakers in many parts of the
world, including Patagonia and the United States, where there were a
quarter of a million Welsh speakers at the end of the nineteenth century. Many thousands of Welsh speakers also moved to English cities,
such as Liverpool and London.

In Wales, however, beginning in the middle of the nineteenth century, the circumstances governing the use of language were largely
damaging to the future of Welsh. English was the only language of
law and administration; in the latter half of that century Welsh was
banned in schools. In spite of this, a national resurgence has seen
Welsh gaining ground once again. A quarter of Wales' primary
schools are Welsh-medium schools. Welsh is now taught as a subject
in almost all schools in Wales, and there are Welsh-language chan-
nels, both on radio and television. Welsh literature, which has an
unbroken tradition going back to AD 600, is flourishing.

Knowing Welsh, therefore, is the key to getting a firsthand expe-
rience of Welsh history and literature. But for the casual visitor, it
is also the key to ensure a warm welcome in many parts of Wales,

as Welsh is still the first language of the most beautiful parts of the country in western and northern Wales.

This book has two parts. The first gives you information about the country (geography, history, economy, culture, fate of the language, and customs and traditions), while the second part consists of language lessons.

The language lessons are designed for a traveller or a non-specialist. You will learn useful phrases and words for special situations as well as basic grammar hints. The lessons will not cover all grammatical problems, nor will they give a rich vocabulary for sophisticated conversation. Nevertheless, they will teach you enough to feel comfortable in a variety of situations, and enough to ensure you are a welcome guest, as the Welsh show great affinity for those interested in their language and culture.

We hope that with this small, compact book you will have in your pocket a collection of bits of information sufficient to carry out satisfying conversations with the people of the country you visit, in their own language. Several U.S. universities teach Welsh, and **Cymdeithas Madog** organizes a weeklong Welsh course annually in the States. Welsh speakers and Welsh lessons are available on the Internet. A useful starting point in the United States is the Web site for **Cymdeithas Madog** (Welsh Studies Institute in North America), www.madog.org, and in Wales, the Welsh Language Board, 5-7 St. Mary's St., Cardiff, CF10 1AT, www.bwrdd-yr-iaith.org.uk.

We wish you good luck in your study and a wonderful trip.

Wales

GEOGRAPHY

Wales is a small country situated to the west of England, and over the sea from Ireland. Its surface area is 20,767 square kilometers (8,016 square miles) and it has a population of approximately 2,959,000 inhabitants. Administratively, Wales has a national assembly,* which decides on matters of home interest, such as education, the economy, health, and welfare. It has some legislative powers, but otherwise sends forty Members of Parliament (MPs) to the London Parliament. In local government, Wales is divided into twenty-two local government authorities.

The country is largely hilly and mountainous. The only lowland areas are the South and North Wales coastal strips, and the island of Anglesey in North Wales. Eighty-one percent of the country is in agricultural use, 12 percent woodland, and 7 percent urban.

The country has several mountain ranges: Snowdonia in the northwest, where Snowdon (3,560 feet) is the highest mountain. Snowdonia has fifteen peaks over three thousand feet. The Cambrian Mountains cover much of mid-Wales, to the east of the seaside and university town of Aberystwyth, and the Brecon Beacons have the highest mountain in South Wales (**Pen y fan**, 2,907 feet). Other ranges include the Preseli Hills in Pembrokeshire, southwest Wales, the Clwydian Hills in northeast Wales, and the Black Mountains of Gwent in southeast Wales. If the territory of Wales were spread flat, the country would be four times its size!

Wales has a beautiful coastline to its north, west and, south, and is linked to England along its eastern border. The coastline has a total of 732 miles, and forms 17 percent of the total British coastline. The longest river is the Severn (220 miles), which runs from its source in the Cambrian Mountains eastwards to England before flowing back

---

*Setting-up date was 1999 after the Welsh voted for establishing it in an historic referendum on 18 September 1997.

along the South Wales coast through the Bristol Channel (called **Môr Hafren** in Welsh—the Severn Sea). There are good fishing rivers flowing towards the sea in western and southern Wales, the **Tywi** (68 miles), flowing through Carmarthen in the south, and **Teifi** (73 miles), flowing through Cardigan in the west. Other rivers flowing partly through England but originating in Wales are the Dee (111 miles), flowing to the sea at the border of Wales and England in the north, and Wye (130 miles), which forms the southeastern border of Wales. There are twenty rivers longer than twenty-five miles, and a total of around fifteen thousand miles of river.

The country has more than four hundred natural lakes and ninety reservoirs. **Llyn Tegid** (4 miles long, 1 mile wide), near Bala in northwest Wales, is the largest natural lake. Others in Mid and North Wales are reservoirs, supplying English cities with cheap water. This has long been a bone of contention, as has been the drowning of Welsh communities. These lakes include **Llyn Celyn, Vyrnwy, Claerwen**, and **Clywedog**. Lake Brianne in the mountains of southern Mid Wales supplies water for Swansea and the surrounding area.

The country is sparsely populated, except for the industrial areas of southeast and northeast Wales. These areas were, for two hundred years, centers of heavy industry, with coal, iron, steel and copper production supplying much of the early wealth and power of the British Empire. In the twentieth century, the number of coal miners fell from a quarter of a million to a few thousand, and many large steel works closed. These industries have, to some extent, been replaced by electronic factories, producing TV sets and computer materials, and by factories producing parts for motor cars.

Some areas, including parts of the main holiday areas of northern and western Wales, have been inundated by English people, buying up homes at the expense of the local people. At the turn of the nineteenth century, scores of thousands of English people, and some from other countries, came to Wales to work in the heavy industries, but most of these have become assimilated and consider themselves Welsh.

Major cities

The largest cities in Wales are Cardiff (321,000 inhabitants), Swansea (225,000), Newport (160,000), Wrexham (125,000), Neath (71,000).

The southeastern valleys, including the towns of Rhondda, Pontypridd, Maesteg, Merthyr Tydfil, and Aberdare have a population of more than half a million.

National parks

Wales has three large areas of national parks: Snowdonia (838 square miles), Pembrokeshire Coast (225 square miles), and Brecon Beacons (519 square miles). There are thirty-two country parks distributed all over the country, and five areas of outstanding natural beauty. Among these are Gower, near Swansea, the first area to be so designated in Britain (1956). Large tracts of coastline are also protected, and Heritage Coast areas form more than 40 percent of the Welsh coast. There are forty-nine National Nature Reserves, and nineteen Local Nature Reserves.

Climate

Wales has a mild climate, without extremes of heat or cold except on the highest mountains. The country has an annual rainfall of around fifty-four inches. Rain can fall at any time, but it is warmer in summer. Snow does not last long in winter (except for about one hundred days a year on the mountains of Snowdonia). The average July temperature is around sixteen degrees Celsius, but in summer temperatures higher than twenty degrees occur regularly. The Gulf Stream from South America keeps the South Wales coast free from frost in winter, and you can comfortably swim in the sea during the summer months.

HISTORY AND POLITICS

Welsh history can be said to have started in the year AD 383, when Magnus Maximus, the Roman ruler, left the country with his armies in the hope of becoming the Roman Emperor. Nevertheless, the seed of Wales had already been sown in the prehistoric era.

Standing stones, dolmens, and stone circles, which dot the countryside, belong to the same period as Stonehenge in England, the stones of which came from the Preseli Mountains in Pembrokeshire. These stone formations, many of which were burial places, others possibly places of religious significance, were built during the pre-Celtic era. Wales consisted of people who had wandered from the Iberian peninsula, that is, Spain, and southern Europe. The Celts, who had inhabited parts of central Europe around Austria, conquered many parts of Europe and took over Rome around 300 BC. They arrived in Britain in several waves from around 800 BC. It was their language and culture that became the languages of the present-day Celtic nations. Welsh (Wales), Breton (Brittany), and Cornish (Cornwall) belong to one branch of these languages, while Irish (Ireland), Gaelic (Scotland), and Manx (Isle of Man) belong to the other.

Between the fourth and sixth centuries AD, Welsh monks preached the Gospel and established churches in many parts of Wales, Ireland, Cornwall, and Brittany. At that time the Welsh were being conquered in England, while the first Welsh poetry which has survived was written around AD 600 in northern England and southern Scotland. This poetry describes Welsh warriors who were defeated in battle. The historic Arthur was probably a Welsh army leader who had considerable success fighting the Anglo-Saxons during this period.

The English kings of the period were anxious to consolidate their gains in England, and one of them, Offa, built an early version of the iron curtain when he built a wall, Offa's Dyke, around AD 780 to keep the Welsh from his kingdom. This dyke has remained more or less the border between Wales and England until today.

From 400 to 1282 the Welsh developed their own system of rulers. Among the earliest was Maelgwn Gwynedd, who ruled in northwest Wales until his death of a plague in 549. Although the country was not often united under one specific ruler, they were united by a common language and literature, a system of laws, codified by King Hywel Dda around 900, and by their common struggle against persistent invaders. Among the kings and princes who united most of the country under their control were Rhodri Mawr (ruled 844–78), the grandfather of Hywel Dda (c. 900–50), and Gruffydd ap Llywelyn (1039–63).

The invaders included Irish, Danes, Vikings, and Norman English. The Normans succeeded in gaining large parts of the country, and Wales' two last great rulers included Llywelyn Fawr the Great (c. 1173–1240) and Llywelyn ap Gruffudd (Llywelyn II, or the Last, c. 1223–82). Two wars of independence were fought, in 1267–77 and 1282–83.

Most of the castles, for example, Harlech, Caernarfon, Conwy, and Beaumares in the north, and Caerphilly, Cardiff, and Kidwelly in the south, which are still a part of Wales' landscape, were built by the Normans, although some, such as Dolbadarn and Dolwyddelan in the north and Dinefwr and Dryslwyn in the south, are of Welsh origin.

The following years were ones of harsh English revenge, but under Owain Glyndŵr the Welsh regained their independence for a brief period from 1400 onwards. After his defeat, the Welsh once again thought that they had won a great victory when Henry VII, of half-Welsh descent, defeated the English king at the Battle of Bosworth (1485), with the help of a Welsh army. This led, nevertheless, to the eventual political annexation of Wales by England with the Acts of Annexation of 1536 and 1542. From then on, English was to be the only language of law and administration. Welsh laws were replaced by English laws, and the Welsh system of government was to become part of the English system.

It was fortunate for the Welsh language, still spoken as the only language by around 95 percent of the population, that in its attempt to create a united Protestant state, the English parliament called for a translation of the Bible and other religious texts into Welsh. This led in future centuries to several mass education movements, so that by the nineteenth century, Wales was a Welsh-speaking, literate country where the language flourished.

During the eighteenth and nineteenth centuries, Nonconformist denominations flourished, taking the place of the established Protestant state church as the main religious organization. These denominations used mainly Welsh and were part of a democratic folk culture, whereas the state church was linked to the ruling landowning and English-orientated classes.

Heavy industries, including quarrying, iron, and coal changed the face of many parts of the country in the nineteenth century. The valleys of South Wales became heavily populated, and at first attracted Welsh speakers from rural areas. It has been argued that this industrialization kept most Welsh people in their own country, and thus safeguarded the language, at a time when there was mass emigration from Europe to America.

When voting rights were given generally to men in the second half of the nineteenth century, Wales turned its back on the English Conservative Party, and was a stronghold for the Liberal Party, which advocated Welsh home rule. One of its leaders, David Lloyd George, became Prime Minister of Britain, and introduced social measures such as state pensions.

During this period of national revival, several national Welsh institutions were established, such as the University of Wales (1893), the National Library of Wales (1907), and the National Museum of Wales (1907). Throughout the twentieth century, the cultural, economic, and political life of Wales came to be organised more on national lines.

With the growth of heavy industries, the Labour Party grew in strength in Wales and became the main party in Wales after the First World War. Unfortunately, until fairly recently, it only paid lip service to Welsh national aspirations, and this led to the formation of **Plaid Cymru** (1925), the national party of Wales, whose aim is self-government for Wales. **Yr Urdd**, the Welsh League of Youth, which has become one of Europe's main youth movements, had been established in 1922.

Since the Second World War there have been many important developments contributing to Welsh nationhood. Among these are the establishment of the Welsh Office (1964), Welsh Books Council (1961), the Welsh Playgroup Movement (1971), Welsh Development Agency (1976), and S4C (the Welsh Television Channel, 1982). One of the most hopeful developments of the last fifty years has been the establishment of around 130 Welsh-medium primary schools in largely English-speaking parts of Wales, mainly through parental demand.

In the general election of 2005, twenty-nine of Wales' forty MPs were Labour Party MPs, four Liberal-Democrat, three Plaid Cymru (Welsh National Party), three Conservative, and one independent.

In the Welsh National Assembly election of 2007, Labour won twenty-six of the sixty seats, Plaid Cymru fifteen, Conservatives twelve, Liberal-Democrat six, and others one.

ECONOMICS

Wales was in the nineteenth century a center of world importance for several industries. But the history of industry in Wales is long. Copper and gold were mined during Roman times, and small deposits of gold are still available in the Dolgellau area in North Wales, and near Pumsaint in South Wales. Coal has been mined regularly since the seventeenth century, and became the main extractive industry in the nineteenth and twentieth centuries. Ironmaking boomed in the nineteenth century, with Merthyr Tydfil in the South Wales valleys the most important center for a considerable period. Steelmaking is still an important industry in South Wales, with the main works at Port Talbot, although several plants have closed in Wales since the 1980s. Tinplate works and copper works were at their peak in the nineteenth century, especially in Swansea, which was once a world center for copper. Copper ore was mined on the island of Anglesey, and slate quarrying became important in North Wales towards the end of the nineteenth century.

Although Welsh communities profited at various times from these industries, the country's wealth has generally been exported to foreign industrialists. Recently new industries, some based in electronics and involved in the production of television sets and other commodities, have been established, but with the availability of cheap labor in eastern Europe and the Far East, many manufacturing factories have closed. Several motor manufacturers have factories that produce engines, gears, and other parts for cars. Once again, most of the wealth created by these industries is sent abroad, including the Far East, rather than kept in Wales.

Farming, the wool trade and cattle rearing have been traditional industries. With the growth of extractive industries, and the need for exporting, the shipping industries became important, and many western coastal towns, such as Porthmadog and Cardigan became centers of shipbuilding. Many of the old ports have become modern-day marinas for small craft. Ports along the south coast, including Cardiff, Barry, and Swansea, had a busy worldwide trade, and developed colorful dockland communities.

Wales is richly blessed in natural resources. It has ample water supplies. Its large coal resources, even if extracted vigorously, could last another three hundred years. Many mineral deposits have been mined, including silver and lead as well as iron, copper, and gold. The country has ample agricultural land, although much of it is in upland areas, and is used for rearing sheep, of which some 12,000,000 are seen roaming in all parts of the country. Coal and water have been used to create electricity, of which there is ample supply through various power stations. Recently, advances have been made using wind power.

The finance and service industries have been developing at a pace, and Cardiff, the capital city, is now a financial and institutional center of importance.

In spite of all these riches, Wales was constantly a country of comparatively high unemployment in the twentieth century. The economic scene was ravaged by the depression of the 1920s and 1930s, when half a million people left the country to find work elsewhere. This led to some valley coal-mining communities having unemployment rates of up to 70 percent. The official unemployment figure for 2006 was 5.2 percent, but as the way of counting these figures has been changed around twenty times for cosmetic effect, the real figure must be double this amount, and in certain parts of the socially deprived industrial valleys and of rural Wales, the figure was far higher.

Nevertheless, much progress has been made in developing the economy in certain parts of Wales, especially the southeast. The Welsh Development Agency, formed in 1976 to tackle some of the worst hit areas but now incorporated into the National Assembly for Wales, succeeded in attracting inward investment, but it was sometimes criticized for concentrating development in the areas nearest to the south and north roads which lead to England, rather than creating a sound infrastructure for the development of an all-Wales economy.

LITERATURE AND ARTS

The first known Welsh poem was written around AD 600, and since then Wales has had an unbroken tradition of Welsh-language literature. The early poets held important posts in the courts of the princes, and were regarded as educators, historians, and entertainers. The important position of the poets under the old order continued after the death of the last of the Welsh princes in 1282, and they became the poets of the gentry. Welsh poetry experienced a golden age from 1300 to 1500, and its most well-known poet, Dafydd ap Gwilym, wrote joyously about love, life, religion, and nature in the fourteenth century.

Wales is also rich in tales. Medieval tales were recounted orally, in a tradition linked with Ireland and other European countries. The best known tales of this period are the **Mabinogi**, or **Mabinogion**. They relate adventures associated with figures of Welsh, Irish, and Roman history and with Celtic deities, and include many folk themes which are in common with the Indo-European tradition.

The translation of the Bible into Welsh in 1588 was an important development, and led to the flowering of modern literature. Hymn writing later gave way to Romantic poetry, the development of the novel, and plays.

One institution which has supported Welsh literature throughout the centuries is the **eisteddfod** (an assembly of Welsh bards, minstrels, and literati), where bards have traditionally competed with each other to win one of two main prizes, the chair and the crown. The first known eisteddfod was held by Lord Rhys ap Gruffudd at Cardigan in 1176. Around 1500, the bards held several important eisteddfodau in order to keep the bardic order and to establish rules of writing poetry. These included the intricate **cynghanedd** (harmony), in which strict rules regarding repetition of consonants and rhyme govern each line of writing. The winner of the chair in the National Eisteddfod, held for a week annually in present-day Wales, must write a poem using these intricate rules.

The golden age of Welsh publishing was the nineteenth century, when a literate populace read avidly. A ten-volume encyclopedia, scores of magazines and newspapers, and hundreds of books on all kinds of subjects were among the products of a successful publishing industry.

The twentieth century saw another period of constantly developing writing. Among the best know writers are Gwenallt (a pacifist Christian nationalist poet), Waldo Williams (who can be similarly defined), Kate Roberts (a novelist and short-story writer on the slate quarry communities), Saunders Lewis (playwright, poet, literary critic), Islwyn Ffowc Elis (novelist), Gwyn Thomas (poet), Gerallt Lloyd Owen (nationalist poet).

Welsh-language arts developed with the advent of radio and television. Welsh-language radio is available all day, and the present Welsh TV channel, S4C, broadcasts over 80 hours of Welsh-language programs each week. In 2009, S4C will become a wholly Welsh-language service in the digital age This has led to popular Welsh soap operas and films. There are around fifty independent television companies operating in Wales, as well as about ten active publishing houses.

Welsh performers have flourished in the musical world, both in traditional opera—the Welsh National Opera Company has won worldwide acclaim—and popular entertainment. Among the prominent names of the second half of the twentieth century are Geraint Evans, Bryn Terfel, (opera), Shirley Bassey, Tom Jones, Harry Secombe, Mary Hopkin, and Katherine Jenkins (singers and entertainers).

There has been a growth in interest in the work of Welsh artists. Richard Wilson and Thomas Jones (eighteenth century) belonged to the Romantic school. Evans Walters (twentieth century) from Swansea was an impressionist painter, depicting many local people and scenes, while Augustus John and his sister Gwen Jones also developed from the impressionist era. Ceri Richards was a foremost symbolist, and Kyffin Williams (1918-2006) was a powerful landscape painter. Other recent notable painters who are part of a new resurgence of Welsh painting include Ceri Richards, and, more recently, Mary Lloyd Jones and Tim Davies.

English-language writing in Wales has, today, also come into its own. The perceived anti-Welsh writings of Caradoc Evans (short stories) and Gwyn Thomas (stories and plays) hindered its acceptance, but Dylan Thomas' fame as a poet has continued to grow. With the nationalist vision of writers such as R.S. Thomas (poet) and other recent writers, English-medium writing in Wales in now a part of Wales' literary tradition.

Welsh popular singing in Welsh and English has developed simultaneously. Dafydd Iwan has been for decades the most popular Welsh folk singer. In the pop scene recent successful groups include the bilingual Super Furry Animals and Catatonia.

FATE OF THE LANGUAGE

According to the 2001 census, 23 percent of the population, 659,301 people, can speak Welsh, and a total of 797,717 people (28 percent of the population) claim to have some knowledge of it. These numbers represent the first increase ever in both the number and percentage of Welsh speakers in almost a century.

But the future of Welsh, just as in the case of several other non-state languages in Europe, is not yet secure. Welsh had from the sixteenth century lost its status as the language of law, government, and administration. Nevertheless, in spite of the 1536 Act of Annexation which aimed at doing away with the language, Welsh flourished as the language of society and religion, especially after the translation of the Bible in 1588. Its use in popular education movements strengthened its position, and it continued to flourish until the mid-nineteenth century in spite of its lack of official status.

A report on education in Wales in 1847 denounced the Welsh for their lack of knowledge in English, at a time when the masters of industry were largely monoglot English. This gave rise to an inferiority complex in the Welsh and a lack of confidence in their own language. Welsh children came to be punished for speaking Welsh in schools, and when, after 1870, primary education was made compulsory, English became the only language of education in Wales. This was followed by mass immigration into Wales of mainly English-speaking people, and by the end of the nineteenth century, the linguistic pattern of Wales was changing rapidly.

During the course of the twentieth century, which started with 50 percent of the people of Wales able to speak Welsh, the position of the Welsh language was further weakened and eroded by economic and political forces. Some 20,000 Welsh speakers were killed in the First World War, and in the following twenty years around 250,000 Welsh speakers emigrated to England and beyond during the years of economic depression. A further six thousand Welsh speakers were killed in the Second World War.

With the advent of mass media, and the continually expanding influence of Anglo-American popular culture, and the ever-centralizing forces of London government and administration, the Welsh language continued to lose ground. English became more and more the language of work, commerce, education, and popular culture. The numbers of Welsh speakers, especially in southeast Wales, fell as Welsh was not spoken in the homes, and the areas which had a majority of Welsh speakers declined.

By the end of the twentieth century, very few places in Wales had more than 80 percent Welsh speakers, although large areas of northern and western Wales still have more than 50 percent Welsh speakers. The notion of a Welsh-speaking Wales is largely attributed to west and north Wales, but this does not take into account the large numbers of Welsh speakers who live in the south. Numerically, more people speak Welsh in South than in North Wales.

To counteract the continual reduction in numbers of Welsh speakers, many Welsh people have strived to set up organizations and bodies that could further the language. One of the most successful is **Urdd Gobaith Cymru**—the Welsh League of Youth—a youth movement established by Ifan ab Owen Edwards in 1922. This movement has attractive youth camps and organizes a hugely successful annual **eisteddfod**.

In 1925 the Welsh national party—**Plaid Cymru**—was founded, with the aim of creating a Welsh-speaking, self-governing country. Although the party did not have much political success before Gwynfor Evans became Member of Parliament for Carmarthen in 1966, it has been a forceful pressure group, and has influenced the political thinking of all parties. It has also fought many successful campaigns which have seen the Welsh language gain a respectable place on radio and television, and as a language of administration.

One of the most successful movements has been the parents, individuals, and bodies who have been responsible for the growth of Welsh-medium and bilingual education. The first Welsh-medium primary schools were established after the Second World War, and by the end of the twentieth century, around 450 primary schools in Wales were teaching through the medium of Welsh. This increase was produced to some extent by the huge popularity of **Mudiad Ysgolion Meithrin**—the Welsh-medium playgroup movement, established in 1971, which now attracts around fifteen thousand children under five years of age to its pre-school playgroups. Secondary education through the medium of Welsh has also flourished, with around fifty schools teaching some subjects through the medium of Welsh, and around twenty-five teaching mainly through the medium of Welsh. By the mid-1990s, Welsh became a compulsory subject in almost all English-medium schools in Wales. The effect of this growth is that 25 percent of Welsh primary schools are now Welsh-medium schools, and there has been an increase of Welsh-speaking children and young people over the last twenty years. This gives sound hope for the future.

The number of adults learning Welsh has also increased annually. Courses are organized by six language centers, which coordinate courses that are run by Wales' colleges and universities. Around twenty thousand attend courses each year, and this number is augmented by those who learn Welsh through popular books, radio, and television programs. CYD is an organization that caters to learners of Welsh throughout the country, organizing social events locally.

Cymdeithas yr Iaith Gymraeg, the Welsh Language Society, was established in 1962 as a pressure group to ensure for Welsh a measure of official status. It adopted non-violent, civil disobedience as a form of action, and this brought swift results. A Welsh Language Act was passed in 1967, and a second Welsh Language Act in 1993. These have ensured that Welsh is used daily by all local authorities and public bodies. Bilingual road signs were the norm by the mid-1970s, and S4C, the partly Welsh television channel (which will become a wholly Welsh channel in 2009), was established in 1982. This movement has attracted much support from young people, and has given rise to popular Welsh music and culture.

Many other movements have supported activities in Welsh, not least the annual Welsh national **eisteddfod**, which lasts a week. Music, poetry, art, prose, singing, and reciting competitions are held daily, with many other activities—for example, a rock music tent—catering to many tastes. The Books Council of Wales, established in the early 1960s, promotes Welsh publishing, and many publishing houses produce between four hundred and five hundred Welsh language books annually. Several recording companies supply a constant stream of Welsh language music. Welsh literature and Welsh-medium culture have flourished in the last forty years.

Welsh is a thriving Celtic language. Indeed, the vigor of Welsh culture and the youth of its speakers augur well for the future.

TIPS FOR SOCIALIZING IN WALES

Welsh people are warm-hearted and humorous, so little formality is needed, even in fairly formal situations. Shake hands on meeting for the first time, but not after this. People will always ask you from where you come, and to whom you may be related, or what personal or local connections you may have, so be eloquent on this. Less important is the work you do.

Some social manners take some time to get used to. If you offer a drink, a Welshman may at first say no in order to be polite. This may be repeated a second time. On the third offer he or she will probably accept. This seems to be in keeping with the adage 'three tries for a

Welshman'. If a Welshman asks a guest if he wants a drink, it usually is a sign that he himself wants one, so don't refuse without making a similar offer.

In pubs, it is usual for one of the guests to buy a drink for his or her friends, if the number is not too great. This favor is then returned, with each guest buying a round in turn.

If you are invited to a Welsh home, don't arrive early, but try to arrive within fifteen minutes. Any gifts you bring, such as small mementos or a bottle of wine, would be most gratefully received.

THE WELSH LANGUAGE AND GRAMMAR

The Welsh language belongs to the Celtic group of languages, which has two branches: Gaelic, Irish, and Manx on one side and Welsh, Breton, and Cornish on the other. It derives from the Indo-European family of languages, along with Germanic, Romance, and many other linguistic groups.

Dialects in Wales today vary according to accent, vocabulary, and construction, although all dialects can be understood by most Welsh speakers. The dialects can be broadly split into North Welsh and South Welsh groups, although this is an oversimplification, as geographic remoteness, caused by mountain ranges, has given rise to many local characteristics.

Standard literary Welsh, boosted by the popular preaching in Nonconformist chapels in the nineteenth and twentieth centuries, is used as the language of broadcasting, public administration, and higher education today. Attempts have been made in recent years to establish a Welsh grammar more akin to the spoken language, although the main elements of vocabulary and syntax between the two are the same. This book follows broadly this more recent grammar.

The one sound in Welsh that is not used in English is the voiceless 'll', pronounced by blowing voicelessly with the tongue and lips in the 'l' position.

Welsh Grammar at a Glance

The verb forms and grammar used in this book are outlined here, with the lessons in which they are introduced:

PRESENT TENSE: LESSONS 1, 2, 3, 4, 5, 6, 7

bod (to be) and all verbs linked to it:
(To introduce verbs, use **'n** or **yn** after these forms.)

Present Tense

rwy / rydw i / wi	I am
rwyt ti	you are
mae e	he / it is
mae hi	she / it is
mae Huw	Hugh is
mae'r plant	the children are
rydyn ni / ry'n ni	we are
rydych chi / ry'ch chi	you are
maen nhw	they are

Question Forms

ydw i?	am I?
wyt ti?	are you?
ydy e?	is he / it?
ydy hi?	is she / it?
ydy Huw?	is Hugh?
ydy'r plant?	are the children?
ydyn ni?	are we?
ydych chi?	are you?
ydyn nhw?	are they?

Negative Forms

dw i ddim	I am not
dwyt ti ddim	you are not
dyw e ddim	he / it is not
dyw hi ddim	she / it is not
dyw Huw ddim	Hugh is not
dyw'r plant ddim	the children are not
dy'n ni ddim	we are not
dy'ch chi ddim	you are not
dy'n nhw ddim	they are not

FUTURE TENSE: LESSON 2

Future Tense

bydd hi	it will be

Question Form

fydd hi?	will it be?

Negative Form

fydd hi ddim	it will not be

PAST TENSE (PERFECT): LESSON 10

Perfect Tense

rwy / rydw i / wi wedi	I have
rwyt ti wedi	you have
mae e wedi	he has
etc.	

Question Forms

ydw i wedi?	have I?
wyt ti wedi?	have you?
etc.	

Negative Forms

dw i ddim wedi	I have not
dwyt ti ddim wedi	you have not
etc.	

PAST TENSE (IMPERFECT): LESSON 13

Imperfect Tense

roeddwn i / ro'n i	I was
roeddet ti / rot ti	you were
roedd e	he / it was
roedd hi	she / it was
roedd Huw	Hugh was
roedd y plant	the children were
roedden ni / ro'n ni	we were
roeddech chi / ro'ch chi	you were
roedden nhw / ro'n nhw	they were

Question Forms

o'n i?	was I?
o't ti?	were you?
oedd e?	was he / it?
oedd hi?	was she / it?
oedd Huw?	was Hugh?
oedd y plant?	were the children?
o'n ni?	were we?
o'ch chi?	were you?
o'n nhw?	were they?

Negative Forms

do'n i ddim	I wasn't
do't ti ddim	you weren't
doedd e ddim	he / it wasn't
doedd hi ddim	she / it wasn't
doedd Huw ddim	Hugh wasn't
doedd y plant ddim	the children weren't
do'n ni ddim	we weren't
do'ch chi ddim	you weren't
do'n nhw ddim	they weren't

PLUPERFECT TENSE: LESSON 13

Pluperfect Tense

ro'n i wedi	I had
ro't ti wedi	you had
roedd e wedi	he / it had
etc.	

Question Forms

o'n i wedi?	had I?
o't ti wedi?	had you?
oedd e wedi?	had he / it?
etc.	

VERB COMMANDS: LESSON 14

Add -**wch** to the stem of the verb:

cysgu	to sleep
cysg**wch**!	go to sleep

VERBS, PAST TENSE, SHORT FORM: LESSON 16

Add the following endings to the stem of the verb:

For example:
codi   to get up

co**des** i	I got up
co**dest** ti	you got up
co**dodd** e	he got up
co**dodd** hi	she got up
co**dodd** Huw	Hugh got up
co**dodd** y plant	the children got up
co**don** ni	we got up
co**doch** chi	you got up
co**don** nhw	they got up

NUMBERS: LESSON 3

1	**un**	6	**chwe(ch)**
2	**dau**	7	**saith**
3	**tri**	8	**wyth**
4	**pedwar**	9	**naw**
5	**pum(p)**	10	**deg**

Numbers are usually followed by a singular noun.

GENDER OF WORDS: LESSON 8

All Welsh nouns are either masculine or feminine. Some can be both. The main differences in use are:

- feminine nouns are soft mutated after the definite article **y** (the)
- adjectives following feminine nouns are soft mutated

ADJECTIVES: LESSON 9

Most adjectives in Welsh follow the noun. Adjectives following feminine nouns soft mutate.

bachgen bach   small boy
merch fach   small girl

MUTATIONS: LESSONS 8, 14

The following changes can occur to the initial letters of words:

Soft Mutation

c > g	g > /	ll > l
p > b	b > f	m > f
t > d	d > dd	rh > r

Aspirate Mutation

c > ch	p > ph	t > th

Nasal Mutation

c > ngh	p > mh	t > nh
g > ng	b > m	d > n

PLURALS: LESSON 11

There are many ways of forming the plurals of Welsh nouns. The most common is adding **-au** to the noun.

PHRASES USING PREPOSITIONS: LESSON 12

Most common prepositions:

i	to	**am**	for
ar	on	**at**	to
gan	by	**heb**	without
o	of, from	**dan**	under
dros	over	**drwy**	through
wrth	by		

POSSESSIVE PRONOUNS: LESSON 14

fy ... i	my	**ein ... ni**	our
dy ... di	your	**eich ... chi**	your
ei ... e	his	**eu ... nhw**	their
ei ... hi	her		

POSSESSIVE PRONOUNS AS OBJECT OF VERBS: LESSON 15

These possessive pronouns, when put around verbs (that is, before and after the verb), become the object of the verb. Note the mutations which occur with these.

For example:
talu	to pay

fy nhalu i	to pay me
dy dalu di	to pay you
ei dalu e	to pay him
ei thalu hi	to pay her
ein talu ni	to pay us
eich talu chi	to pay you
eu talu nhw	to pay them

Noun Clauses: Lesson 15

'That' is translated by **bod**. The possessive pronouns put around **bod** are used to express pronouns:

fy mod i	that I am
dy fod di	that you are
ei fod e	that he is
ei bod hi	that she is
bod Huw	that Hugh is
bod y plant	that the children are
ein bod ni	that we are
eich bod chi	that you are
eu bod nhw	that they are

Passive Use of Verbs: Lesson 17

'To be (paid)' is translated by **cael**. The possessive pronoun is put around **cael**:

For example:
talu	to pay

rwy'n cael fy nhalu	I'm being paid
rwyt ti'n cael dy dalu	you're being paid
mae e'n cael ei dalu	he's being paid
mae hi'n cael ei thalu	she's being paid
mae Huw'n cael ei dalu	Hugh's being paid
mae'r plant yn cael eu talu	the children are being paid
ry'n ni'n cael ein talu	we're being paid
ry'ch chi'n cael eich talu	you're being paid
maen nhw'n cael eu talu	they're being paid

Pronunciation Guide

Welsh is a fairly phonetic language: most letters have just one sound, while others vary comparatively little. A main difference from English is that it has seven vowel letters (**a, e, i, o, u, w, y**). Another is that it has eight combination letters that stand for one sound (**ch, dd, ff, ng, ll, ph, rh, th**).

The accent on almost all Welsh words is on the last syllable but one. The few exceptions include words which have an **h** before the last syllable (e.g. mwynhau – enjoy) and where the accent is noted by ^, or ` (e.g. caniatâd – permission). The use of ^ on the last syllable of words denotes that the accent is on the last syllable, and that the vowel sound is long.

THE WELSH ALPHABET

Consonants

	English equivalent	Welsh	Pronunciation	Meaning
b	b	**baban**	*bahban*	baby
c	k	**ci**	*kee*	dog
ch	ch (as in lo**ch**)	**chweeh**	*chooehch*	six
d	d	**dyn**	*deen*	man
dd	th (voiced, as in **th**at)	**dydd**	*deeth*	day
f	v	**fi**	*vee*	me
ff	ff (as in o**ff**)	**fferm**	*ffehrm*	farm
g	g (hard as in **g**ame)	**gardd**	*gahrth*	garden
ng	usually ng (as in wi**ng**)	**angladd**	*ahnglath*	funeral
	n-g (as in a**ng**ry)	**Bangor**	*Ban-gor*	Bangor
h	h	**haul**	*haheel*	sun
j	j	**jam**	*jam*	jam
l	l	**lôn**	*loan*	lane
ll	ll	**lle**	*lleh*	place

(position mouth for 'l' and blow voicelessly)

m	m	mam	*mam*	mother
n	n	ni	*nee*	we
p	p	plant	*plant*	children
ph	ff	traphont	*traffont*	viaduct
r	r (trilled)	radio	*rahdyo*	radio
rh	rh (trilled with h)	rhaff	*rhahff*	spade
s	s (as in soon)	seren	*sehrehn*	star
t	t	tŷ	*tee*	house
th	th (voiceless, as in thing)	cath	*kahth*	cat

Vowels

	English equivalent	Welsh	Pronunciation	Meaning
a	a (short, as in America)	dant	*dant*	tooth
	ah (long, as in park)	tân	*tahn*	fire
e	e (short, as in went)	pert	*pert*	pretty
	eh (long, as in café)	peth	*pehth*	thing
	ee (as in week) after 'a'	mae	*mahee*	there is
	after 'o'	oes?	*ohees*	is there?
i	i (short, as in pin)	pin	*pin*	pin
	ee (long, as in week)	sgrîn	*sgreen*	screen
o	o (short, as in gone)	ton	*ton*	wave
	oa (long, as in fore)	côr	*coar*	choir
u	i (short, as in pin)	gwefus	*gooehvis*	lip
	ee (long, as in week)	un	*een*	one
	French 'u'	pur	*'pur'*	pure
	(in North Wales only)			
w	oo (short as in pull)	hwn	*hoon*	this
	oo (long, as in fool)	cŵn	*koon*	dogs
y	i (short, as in pin)	hyn	*hin*	these
	uh (as in fun)	gyrru	*guhree*	to drive
	ee (long, as in week)	dyn	*deen*	man

(In North Wales this **y** is pronounced like the French 'u')

Other combinations

English equivalent		Welsh	Pronunciation	Meaning
si	sh	**siop**	*shop*	shop
wy	ooee	**wy**	*ooee*	egg
sh	sh	**brwsh**	*broosh*	brush

Some words sound similar to English and mean the same:

Welsh	English		Welsh	English
bag	bag		**lifft**	lift
banc	bank		**lili**	lily
beic	bike		**map**	map
camera	camera		**marmalêd**	marmalade
casét	cassette		**mat**	mat
cês	case		**nonsens**	nonsense
cic	kick		**pac**	pack
cloc	clock		**pas**	pass
desg	desk		**pinc**	pink
eliffant	elephant		**pot**	pot
fforc	fork		**problem**	problem
ffresh	fresh		**record**	record
gêm	game		**sgrîn**	screen
golff	golf		**sinema**	cinema
inc	ink		**tic**	tick
jam	jam		**tun**	tin
jîns	jeans		**winc**	wink
lamp	lamp			

Some words sound fairly similar to English and mean the same:

Welsh	Pronunciation	Meaning
basged	*bahsged*	basket
bws	*boos*	bus
carped	*kahrped*	carpet
palas	*pahlahs*	palace
papur	*pahpir*	paper
peint	*peheent*	pint
radio	*rahdyo*	radio
stryd	*streed*	street
traffig	*traffig*	traffic
trên	*trehn*	train
theatr	*thehatr*	theater

Some words sound similar to English but have a different meaning:

Welsh	Pronunciation	Meaning
crap	*crap*	smattering
cul	*keel*	narrow
dim	*dim*	nothing
dyn	*dean*	man
ffrog	*frog*	frock
haws	*house*	easier
hi	*he*	she
hy	*he*	bold
hynt	*hint*	journey
lôn	*loan*	lane
mil	*meal*	thousand
min	*mean*	edge
pump	*pimp*	five
tri	*tree*	three
tyn	*tin*	tight

Some personal names are pronounced similarly:

Welsh	English
Beti	Betty
Efa	Eva
Ffransis	Francis
Gruffudd	Griffith
Henri	Henry
Huw	Hugh
Rhys	Rees

Pronunciation of place names in Wales and their English equivalent:

Welsh	Pronunciation	English
Abertawe	*Ahbehrtahooeh*	Swansea
Aberteifi	*Ahbehrteheevee*	Cardigan
Caerdydd	*Kaheer-deeth*	Cardiff
Caerfyrddin	*Kaheervuhrthin*	Carmarthen
Cei Newydd	*Kehee Nehooith*	New Quay
Cydweli	*Kidwehlee*	Kidwelly
Dinbych	*Dinbich*	Denbigh
Hwlffordd	*Hoolforth*	Haverfordwest
Môn	*Moan*	Anglesey
Pen y Bont	*Pen uh Bont*	Bridgend
Talacharn	*Talahcharn*	Laugharne
Trallwng	*Tralloong*	Welshpool
Tyddewi	*Tee Thehooee*	St. David's

GWERS UN

LESSON ONE

DEIALOG 1: CWRDD

Huw: Shwmae!
Janet: Helo! Bore da!
Huw: Bore da! Shwd ych chi?
Janet: Yn dda iawn. Shwd ych chi?
Huw: Yn dda iawn. Ydych chi'n deall Cymraeg?
Janet: Ydw, tipyn bach. Ydych chi'n siarad Cymraeg?
Huw: Ydw, rwy'n siarad Cymraeg. Ydych chi'n siarad Cymraeg?
Janet: Ydw, tipyn bach.
Huw: Falch i gwrdd â chi.
Janet: Falch i gwrdd â chi hefyd.

DEIALOG 2

Alun: Noswaith dda!
Sian: Noswaith dda!
Alun: Aha! Ydych chi'n siarad Cymraeg?
Sian: Ydw, tipyn bach. Ond siaradwch yn araf.
Alun: Sut dach chi?
Sian: Beth?
Alun: Sut dach chi? Shwd ych chi?
Sian: O! Shwd ych chi! Yn dda iawn diolch. A shwd ych chi?
Alun: Rwy'n dda iawn, diolch!
Sian: Hwyl!
Alun: Pob hwyl!

DIALOGUE 1: MEETING

Hugh: Hello!

Janet: Hello! Good morning!

Hugh: Good morning! How are you?

Janet: Very well. How are you?

Hugh: Very well. Do you understand Welsh?

Janet: Yes, a little. Do you speak Welsh?

Hugh: Yes, I speak Welsh. Do you speak Welsh?

Janet: Yes, a little.

Hugh: Pleased to meet you.

Janet: Pleased to meet you too.

DIALOGUE 2

Alun: Good evening!

Jane: Good evening!

Alun: Aha! Do you speak Welsh?

Jane: Yes, a little. But speak slowly.

Alun: How are you?

Jane: What?

Alun: How are you? How are you?

Jane: Oh! How are you! Very well, thanks. And how are you?

Alun: I'm very well, thanks.

Jane: Good-bye!

Alun: Good-bye!

YMADRODDION A GEIRFA / PHRASES AND VOCABULARY

Helo.	Hello.
Shwmae.	Hello. (South Wales)
Sut 'dach chi?	How are you? (North Wales)
Shwd ych chi?	How are you? (South Wales)
Falch i gwrdd â chi.	Pleased to meet you.
Yn dda iawn.	Very well.
Bore da.	Good morning.
Prynhawn da.	Good afternoon.
Noswaith dda.	Good evening.
Nos da.	Good night.
Ydych chi'n siarad … ?	Do you speak … ?
Ydw.	Yes (I do).
Rwy'n deall Cymraeg.	I understand Welsh.
Na.	No.
Hwyl!	Good-bye!
Pob hwyl!	Good-bye!

GRAMADEG / GRAMMAR

Ydych	chi	'n	siarad	Cymraeg?
Do	you		speak	Welsh?

The **'n** following **chi** introduces the verb **siarad** (speak). It has no meaning of its own, except for continuing the tense (time) of the original verb **ydych** (do).

The above table can be extended to include more languages:

Ydych chi'n siarad Do you speak	Cymraeg (Welsh)? Saesneg (English)? Ffrangeg (French)? Almaeneg (German)? Sbaeneg (Spanish)? Eidaleg (Italian)?

| Ydw. | Yes (I do). |
| Na. | No. |

To say 'I speak' use **Rwy** or **Rydw i** instead of **Ydych**:

Rwy		'n	siarad	Cymraeg
Rydw	i	'n		
I speak Welsh				
or I am speaking Welsh				

This can be extended to include other verbs and to include more languages:

Rwy		'n	siarad	Cymraeg
Rydw	i		deall	Ffrangeg
				Almaeneg
				Sbaeneg
				Eidaleg

| siarad | speak |
| deall | understand |

GEIRFA YCHWANEGOL / ADDITIONAL VOCABULARY

deall	(to) understand
tipyn bach	a little
cwrdd	(to) meet
diolch	thanks
a	and
siaradwch	talk
yn araf	slowly
beth	what

YMARFERION / EXERCISES

1. Read the Welsh aloud several times. Practice with a friend if possible.

2. Cover the English side. Translate the Welsh. Check after each sentence, then attempt it all. Do this several times.

3. Cover the Welsh side. Translate the English. Check after each sentence, then attempt it all. Do this several times.

4. Make up as many questions as you can, selecting words from each column:

Ydych	chi'n	siarad deall	Cymraeg? Ffrangeg? Saesneg? Eidaleg? Sbaeneg? Almaeneg?

5. Answer the questions you have made, by choosing the appropriate answer from this list:

Ydw, rwy'n gallu siarad Cymraeg.
Ydw, tipyn bach.
Na.
Ydw, rwy'n deall Eidaleg.

6. Say which languages you speak or understand:

For example:
Rwy'n siarad Almaeneg.
Rwy'n deall Ffrangeg.

Rwy'n	deall siarad	Ffrangeg Almaeneg Saesneg Eidaleg Sbaeneg Cymraeg

Extra Grammar

1. What is _____ in Welsh?

Beth yw _____ yn Cymraeg?

For example:
Beth yw 'sausage' yn Cymraeg?
Beth yw 'Wales' yn Cymraeg?

2.

I	don't	understand	Welsh.
Dw i	**ddim yn**	**deall**	**Cymraeg.**

I	don't	speak	Welsh.
Dw i	**ddim yn**	**siarad**	**Cymraeg.**

GWERS DAU

LESSON TWO

Deialog 1: Y Tywydd

Sian: Bore da!
Huw: Bore da! Mae hi'n braf.
Sian: Ydy, mae hi'n braf iawn.
Huw: Mae hi'n heulog heddiw.
Sian: Mae hi'n heulog iawn.
Huw: Mae hi'n bwrw glaw yn Aberystwyth.
Sian: Ond mae hi'n braf yn Abertawe.

Deialog 2

Alun: Noswaith dda, Mari.
Mari: Noswaith dda, Alun. Shwd ych chi?
Alun: Yn dda iawn. Fydd hi'n braf heno?
Mari: Bydd, bydd hi'n braf iawn.
Alun: Fydd hi'n braf yfory?
Mari: Na, bydd hi'n bwrw glaw.
Alun: O daro!

Radio: Bydd hi'n sych heno.
        Bydd hi'n bwrw glaw yn y bore.
        Bydd hi'n braf yn y prynhawn.
        Bydd hi'n oer yn y nos.

DIALOGUE 1: THE WEATHER

Sian: Good morning!
Huw: Good morning! It's fine.
Sian: Yes, it's very fine.
Huw: It's sunny today.
Sian: It's very sunny.
Huw: It's raining in Aberystwyth.
Sian: But it's fine in Swansea.

DIALOGUE 2

Alun: Good evening, Mari.
Mary: Good evening, Alun. How are you?
Alun: Very well. Will it be fine tonight?
Mary: Yes, it will be very fine.
Alun: Will it be fine tomorrow?
Mary: No, it will rain.
Alun: Oh dear!

Radio: It will be dry tonight.
        It will rain in the morning.
        It will be fine in the afternoon.
        It will be cold in the night.

YMADRODDION A GEIRFA / PHRASES AND VOCABULARY

mae hi'n	it is
bydd hi'n	it will be
bwrw glaw	raining
braf	fine
oer	cold
sych	dry
heulog	sunny
bwrw eira	snowing
dwym	warm
gymylog	cloudy

GRAMADEG / GRAMMAR

Form of verb 'to be'	Subject	'n	Verb or adjective
Mae	hi	'n	bwrw glaw.
It is raining.			
Mae	hi	'n	bwrw eira.
It is snowing.			
Mae	hi	'n	braf.
It is fine.			

Question and answer

Ydy hi'n bwrw glaw?	**Ydy.**
Is it raining?	Yes.
Ydy hi'n sych?	**Na.**
Is it dry?	No.

Future

Bydd	hi	'n	bwrw glaw.

It will be raining.

Bydd	hi	'n	sych.

It will be dry.

Question and answer

Fydd hi'n braf yfory?	**Bydd.**
Will it be fine tomorrow?	Yes.

Fydd hi'n bwrw glaw yfory?	**Na.**
Will it rain tomorrow?	No.

GEIRFA YCHWANEGOL / ADDITIONAL VOCABULARY

iawn	very
heddiw	today
yn	in
heno	tonight
yfory	tomorrow
daro!	dear!
y nos	the night
bore ma	this morning

YMARFERION / EXERCISES

1. Read the Welsh aloud several times. Practice with a friend if possible.

2. Cover the English side. Translate the Welsh. Check after each sentence, then attempt it all. Do this several times.

3. Cover the Welsh side. Translate the English. Check after each sentence, then attempt it all. Do this several times.

4. Make up as many sentences as you can, selecting words from each column:

Mae Bydd	hi'n	bwrw glaw sych braf oer bwrw eira	heno heddiw yfory yn y nos yn y bore yn y prynhawn bore ma

5. Ask questions on the weather, using:

    Ydy hi'n ... ?
or **Fydd hi'n ... ?**

For example:
Ydy hi'n bwrw glaw heddiw?
Ydy.

Fydd hi'n sych yfory?
Bydd.

Extra Grammar

1. Note that 'it' is translated by **hi** (she) when the weather is discussed. In other instances, 'it' is translated by **hi** (she) when referring to feminine nouns, and by **e** (he) when referring to masculine nouns.

2. Saying 'it isn't':

Negative verb	Subject	Not	yn	Verb
Dyw	**hi**	**ddim**	**yn**	**bwrw glaw**

It is not raining.

Dyw hi ddim yn sych.	It isn't dry.
Dyw hi ddim yn heulog.	It isn't sunny.
Dyw hi ddim yn oer.	It isn't cold.

GWERS TRI

LESSON THREE

DEIALOG 1: YN YR ORSAF

Mae Janet yn cyrraedd Bangor. Mae hi yn yr orsaf. Mae hi yn y swyddfa docynnau.

Janet: Pryd mae'r trên yn mynd i Abertawe?
Mr. Evans: Mae'r trên yn mynd i Abertawe am saith o'r gloch.
Janet: O da iawn. Pryd mae'r trên yn cyrraedd Abertawe?
Mr. Evans: Mae e'n cyrraedd Abertawe am saith o'r gloch y nos.
Janet: O wel, ga i un tocyn i Abertawe?
Mr. Evans: Dychwel?
Janet: Na, un ffordd.
Mr. Evans: Tri deg punt.
Janet: O ble mae'r trên yn mynd?
Mr. Evans: Mae'r trên yn mynd o blatfform tri.

DEIALOG 2

Mae Sian yn yr orsaf bysiau yn Aberystwyth.

Sian: Pryd mae'r bws yn mynd i Abertawe?
Mr. Davies: Mae'r bws yn mynd i Abertawe am un o'r gloch.
Sian: Pryd mae e'n cyrraedd?
Mr. Davies: Mae e'n cyrraedd am bedwar o'r gloch.
Sian: Dau docyn i Abertawe, os gwelwch yn dda.
Mr. Davies: Dychwel?
Sian: Na, un ffordd.
Mr. Davies: Un deg wyth punt.
Sian: Ble mae'r bws?
Mr. Davies: Mae'r bws fan hyn.

DIALOGUE 1: AT THE STATION

Janet arrives at Bangor. She is at the station. She is in the booking office (ticket office).

Janet:	When does the train go to Swansea?
Mr. Evans:	The train goes to Swansea at seven o'clock.
Janet.	Oh very good. When does the train arrive at Swansea?
Mr. Evans:	The train arrives at Swansea at seven o'clock at night.
Janet:	Oh well, may I have one ticket to Swansea?
Mr. Evans:	Return?
Janet:	No, one way.
Mr. Evans:	Thirty pounds.
Janet:	From where does the train go?
Mr. Evans:	The train goes from platform three.

DIALOGUE 2

Jane is in the bus station at Aberystwyth.

Jane:	When does the bus go to Swansea?
Mr. Davies:	The bus goes to Swansea at one o'clock.
Jane:	When does it arrive?
Mr. Davies:	It arrives at four o'clock.
Jane:	Two tickets to Swansea, please.
Mr. Davies:	Return?
Jane:	No, one way.
Mr. Davies:	Eighteen pounds.
Jane:	Where is the bus?
Mr. Davies:	The bus is here.

YMADRODDION A GEIRFA / PHRASES AND VOCABULARY

pryd?	when?
sut?	how?
ble?	where?
beth?	what?
'r	the
ga i	may I have
tocyn	ticket
un tocyn	one ticket
dau docyn	two tickets
tri thocyn	three tickets
trên	train
bws	bus
tacsi	taxi
awyren	airplane
un ffordd	one way
dychwel	return
mynd	(to) go
dod	(to) come
aros	(to) stay, (to) stop
gadael	(to) leave
cyrraedd	(to) arrive (at)
newid	change
prynu	(to) buy
rhaid	must
punt	pound

GRAMADEG / GRAMMAR

Forming questions

Question word	Form of verb 'to be'	Subject	yn or 'n	Verb
Pryd	**mae**	**'r trên**	**yn**	**mynd?**
When is the train going?				
Ble	**mae**	**'r bws**	**yn**	**aros?**
Where does the bus stop?				
Sut	**mae**	**Sian**	**yn**	**dod?**
How is Jane coming?				
Ble	**mae**	**'r orsaf?**		
Where is the station?				
Pryd	**mae**	**'r bws**	**yn**	**gadael?**
When does the bus leave?				

GEIRFA YCHWANEGOL / ADDITIONAL VOCABULARY

am	at
o'r gloch	o'clock
wedyn	then
platfform	platform
fan hyn	here

NUMBERS

1	un	11	un deg un (un ar ddeg)	21	dau ddeg un
2	dau	12	un deg dau (deuddeg)	22	dau ddeg dau
3	tri	13	un deg tri	23	dau ddeg tri
4	pedwar	14	un deg pedwar	24	dau ddeg pedwar
5	pump	15	un deg pump (pymtheg)	25	dau ddeg pump
6	chwech	16	un deg chwech	26	dau ddeg chwech
7	saith	17	un deg saith	27	dau ddeg saith
8	wyth	18	un deg wyth (deunaw)	28	dau ddeg wyth
9	naw	19	un deg naw	29	dau ddeg naw
10	deg	20	dau ddeg (ugain)	30	tri deg

31	tri deg un	70	saith deg	300	tri chant
40	pedwar deg	71	saith deg un	400	pedwar cant
41	pedwar deg un	80	wyth deg	500	pum cant
50	pum deg	81	wyth deg un	600	chwe chant
51	pum deg un	90	naw deg	700	saith cant
60	chwe deg	91	naw deg un	800	wyth cant
61	chwe deg un	100	cant	900	naw cant
		200	dau gant	1000	mil

Numbers in brackets are used with time. Numbers are usually followed by singular nouns:

£5	pum punt
£30	tri deg punt

Ymarferion / Exercises

1. Read the Welsh aloud several times.

2. Cover the English side. Translate the Welsh. Check after each sentence, then attempt it all. Do this several times.

3. Cover the Welsh side. Translate the English. Check after each sentence, then attempt it all. Do this several times.

4. Make up as many questions as you can, selecting words from each column:

Pryd	mae'r	trên	yn mynd?
		bws	yn gadael?
			yn cyrraedd?

5. Give the answers in Welsh:

    a) **Pryd mae'r trên ym mynd i Aberystwyth?** 8 o'clock

    For example:
    Mae'r trên yn mynd i Aberystwyth am wyth o'r gloch.

    b) **Pryd mae'r trên yn gadael Bangor?**   7 o'clock

    c) **Pryd mae'r bws yn gadael Caerdydd?**   1 o'clock

    d) **Pryd mae'r bws yn gadael Llanelli?**   6 o'clock

    e) **Pryd mae'r tên yn mynd i Abertawe?**   9 o'clock

GWERS PEDWAR

LESSON FOUR

Deialog: Cyflwyno

Mae Janet yn dod o Poultney, Vermont. Mae hi'n awr yn Abertawe. Mae hi ar wyliau. Mae hi'n mynd i'r Clwb Cymraeg yn Abertawe.

Mair:	Noswaith dda. Shwd ych chi heno?
Janet:	Noswaith dda! Yn dda iawn, diolch. A chi?
Mair:	Yn dda iawn. Ydych chi'n dod o Abertawe?
Janet:	Na! Janet Evans ydw i. Rwy'n dod o America.
Mair:	O America?
Janet:	Ie. Rwy'n dod o Poultney, Vermont.
Mair:	Beth ydych chi'n gwneud yn Abertawe?
Janet:	Wel, rydw i yma ar wyliau. Rydw i'n moyn dysgu Cymraeg.
Mair:	Croeso i Abertawe! Falch i gwrdd â chi!
Janet:	Ydych chi'n byw yn Abertawe?
Mair:	Ydw. Mair Evans ydw i. Rwy'n byw yma ers pum mlynedd.
Janet:	Ydych chi'n gweithio yma?
Mair:	Ydw. Llyfrgellydd ydw i. Rwy'n gweithio yn y llyfrgell yn Abertawe. A chi? Ydych chi'n gweithio?
Janet:	Ydw. Nyrs ydw i. Rydw i'n gweithio yn yr ysbyty yn Fairhaven. Rwy'n hoffi'r gwaith.
Mair:	Ydych chi'n dod o Vermont?
Janet:	Na, rwy'n dod o Kentucky. Ond mae Mam yn dod o Gymru—mae hi'n dod o Abertawe.
Mair:	O ble yn Abertawe?
Janet:	O'r Mwmbwls. Mae hi'n byw yn America ers hanner can mlynedd, ond mae hi'n hoffi dod i Abertawe ar wyliau.
Mair:	Ydych chi'n nabod rhywun yn Abertawe?

DIALOGUE: INTRODUCTIONS

Janet comes from Poultney, Vermont. She is now in Swansea. She is on holiday. She goes to the Welsh Club in Swansea.

Mair: Good evening. How are you tonight?

Janet: Good evening. Very well, thanks. And you?

Mair: Very well. Do you come from Swansea?

Janet: No! I'm Janet Evans. I come from America.

Mair: From America?

Janet: Yes. I come from Poultney, Vermont.

Mair: What are you doing in Swansea?

Janet: Well, I am here on holiday. I want to learn Welsh.

Mair: Welcome to Swansea! Glad to meet you!

Janet: Do you live in Swansea?

Mair: Yes. I'm Mair Jones. I've lived here for five years.

Janet: Do you work here?

Mair: Yes. I am a librarian. I work in the library in Swansea. And you? Do you work?

Janet: Yes. I am a nurse. I work in the hospital in Fairhaven. I like the work.

Mair: Do you come from Vermont?

Janet: No, I come from Kentucky. But Mom comes from Wales— she comes from Swansea.

Mair: From where in Swansea?

Janet: From the Mumbles. She has lived in America for fifty years, but she likes to come to Swansea on holiday.

Mair: Do you know anyone in Swansea?

Janet: Na, ond rydw i'n mynd i chwilio am achau'r teulu yn y
llyfrgell. Ac rydw i'n mynd i weld popeth! Rydw i'n hoffi
nofio, felly rydw i'n mynd i nofio yn y môr bob dydd.
Rydw i'n hoffi'r theatr, ac rydw i'n hoffi gweld ffilmiau.

Mair: Dewch i'r llyfrgell gyda fi yfory!

Janet: No, but I'm going to search for the family tree in the library. And I'm going to see everything! I like swimming, so I'm going to swim in the sea each day. I like the theater, and I like to see films.

Mair: Come to the library with me tomorrow!

YMADRODDION A GEIRFA / PHRASES AND VOCABULARY

diolch	thanks
diolch yn fawr	thank you very much
os gwelwch yn dda	please
Huw ydw i.	I am Hugh.
Dyma Sian.	Here is Sian.
Ydych chi'n nabod Sian?	Do you know Sian?
Clerc ydw i.	I am a clerk.
Ble ry'ch chi'n byw?	Where do you live?
Rwy'n byw yn Abertawe.	I live in Swansea.

GRAMADEG / GRAMMAR

Word order of Welsh sentences, present tense:

Form of verb 'to be'	Subject	yn (or 'n)	Verb	Object
Rydw	i	'n	hoffi	ffilmiau.

I like films.

Rwyt	ti	'n	hoffi	theatr.

You like theater.

Mae	e	'n	hoffi	Abertawe.

He likes Swansea.

Mae	hi	'n	hoffi	Vermont.

She likes Vermont.

Mae	Sian	yn	hoffi	byw yma.

Sian likes living here.

Rydyn	ni	'n	hoffi	nofio.

We like to swim.

Rydych	chi	'n	hoffi	mynd.

We like to go.

Maen	nhw	'n	hoffi	dod.

They like to come.

Alternative forms, often heard (*pronunciations in italics*)

Rydw i'n	→	Rwy'n
ruhdoo een		*rooeen*
Rydyn ni'n	→	Ry'n ni'n
ruhdin neen		*reen neen*
Rydych chi'n	→	Ry'ch chi'n
ruhdich cheen		*reech cheen*
Dw i'n	→	Wi'n
doo een		*ooeen*

GEIRFA YCHWANEGOL / ADDITIONAL VOCABULARY

noswaith	evening
dda	good [adjectives follow the noun]
heno	tonight
dod	(to) come
na	no
ie	yes
o	from
beth	what
gwneud	(to) do, (to) make
yma	here
ar wyliau	on holiday
moyn	(to) want
dysgu	(to) learn
Cymraeg	Welsh
Croeso	Welcome
i	to
Abertawe	Swansea
byw	(to) live
ers	for, since
pum mlynedd	five years
gweithio	(to) work

ydw	yes (I am)
ydw	I am
yn	in
llyfrgellydd	librarian
llyfrgell	library
a / ac [ac before vowels]	and
nyrs	nurse
ysbyty	hospital
hoffi	(to) like
Mam	Mom
ble	where
hanner can	half a hundred, fifty
mynd	(to) go
nofio	(to) swim
y	the
môr	sea
bob dydd	every day
gweld	(to) see
theatr	theater
ffilmiau	films
wrth gwrs	of course
chwilio	(to) look for, (to) search
achau'r teulu	family tree
popeth	everything
dewch!	come!
gyda fi	with me

YMARFERION / EXERCISES

1. Read the Welsh aloud several times.

2. Cover the English side. Translate the Welsh. Check after each sentence, then attempt it all. Do this several times.

3. Cover the Welsh side. Translate the English. Check after each sentence, then attempt it all. Do this several times.

4. Make up as many sensible sentences as you can, selecting words from each column:

Examples:

Rydw i'n hoffi mynd i'r llyfrgell.	I like going to the library.
Mae hi'n hoffi gweithio yn Abertawe.	She likes working in Swansea.

Rydw i'n (I)	**hoffi**	**nofio**	**yn y môr**
		gweld ffilmiau	yn y sinema
		mynd	i'r theatr
Mae hi'n (She)			ar wyliau
			i'r llyfrgell
		gweithio	yn y llyfrgell
Rydyn ni'n (We)		dysgu Cymraeg	
		byw	yn America
			yn Abertawe
Maen nhw'n (They)			

5. Say what you are:

For example:
Nyrs ydw i.

Here is a short list of occupations:

rheolwr – manager
ysgrifenyddes – secretary
athro – teacher (m)
darlithydd – lecturer
ffermwr – farmer
athrawes – teacher (f)
gyrrwr – driver
technegydd – technician
siopwr – shopkeeper
myfyriwr – student
trydanwr – electrician
gwraig tŷ – housewife
clerc – clerk
pensiynwr – pensioner
di-waith – unemployed
gweithiwr cymdeithasol – social worker

Extra Grammar

1. Familiar and polite forms:

Ti is used for 'you' (singular) when talking to friends, family and children.

Chi is used for 'you' (singular) when talking to all other people.

Chi is also used for 'you' (plural).

2. Use of **yn**:

Yn or **'n** is used to introduce nouns and adjectives; it is not used before prepositions:

Rydw i'n gweld ffilm.	I see a film *or* I am seeing a film.
Rydw i ar wyliau.	I am on holiday.

3. **Ydw** and **ydy** or **yw**:

Ydw is used to link the complement (rather like an = sign) to the subject 'I' (note that the English word order is reversed in Welsh):

Nyrs ydw i.	I am a nurse.

Ydy or **yw** is used to to link the complement to the subject 'he' or 'she':

Llyfrgellydd yw hi.	She is a librarian.
Nyrs yw e.	He is a nurse.

GWERS PUMP

LESSON FIVE

DEIALOG: HOLI'R FFORDD

Mae Janet yn Abertawe. Mae hi'n chwilio am y llyfrgell, ac mae hi ar goll.

Janet:	Esgudosdwch fi. Rydw i ar goll. Ydych chi'n gwybod ble mae'r llyfrgell?
Dafydd:	Ydw, ry'ch chi'n bell iawn. Y'ch chi'n gwybod ble mae'r stryd fawr?
Janet:	Ydw, wrth gwrs.
Dafydd:	Wel, ewch i'r stryd fawr, wedyn ewch i'r chwith, ac wedyn yn syth ymlaen. Wrth y gwesty, trowch i'r chwith eto, ac wedyn i'r dde …
Janet:	Arhoswch! Rydw i ar goll nawr. Ydw i'n troi i'r chwith wrth y gwesty?
Dafydd:	Ydych. Ydych chi'n gwybod ble mae Gwesty Forte?
Janet:	Ydw, wrth y gylchfan.
Dafydd:	Ie, wel, i'r chwith wrth y gwesty, wedyn i'r dde, ar hyd Heol Alexandra, ac mae'r llyfrgell ar y dde.
Janet:	Diolch yn fawr i chi.

Mae Janet yn cerdded i'r stryd fawr, ac wedyn mae hi'n troi i'r chwith. Wedyn maen hi'n troi i'ch chwith, ond wedyn mae hi ar goll. Mae Janet yn gweld tacsi. Mae hi'n codi llaw:

Janet:	Tacsi!
Gyrrwr tacsi:	Ie? Ble rydych chi'n mynd?
Janet:	Rwy'n mynd i'r llyfrgell. Ydych chi'n gallu mynd â fi?
Gyrrwr tacsi:	Ydw, wrth gwrs, dim problem. Mae'r llyfrgell yn agos—mae hi'n agos iawn. Ydych chi'n dod o Abertawe?
Janet:	Na, rwy'n dod o Vermont.

DIALOGUE: ASKING THE WAY

Janet is in Swansea. She is looking for the library, and she is lost.

Janet:	Excuse me. I am lost. Do you know where the library is?
Dafydd:	Yes, you're very far. Do you know where the high street is?
Janet:	Yes, of course.
Dafydd:	Well, go to the high street, then go to the left, and then straight on. By the hotel, turn to the left again, and then to the right …
Janet:	Wait! I'm lost now. Do I turn to the left by the hotel?
Dafydd:	Yes. Do you know where Forte Hotel is?
Janet:	Yes, by the roundabout.
Dafydd:	Yes, well, to the left by the hotel, then to the right, along Alexandra Road, and the library is on the right.
Janet:	Thank you very much.

Janet walks to the high street and then she turns to the left. Then she turns to the left, and then she is lost. She sees a taxi. She raises a hand:

Janet:	Taxi!
Taxi driver:	Yes? Where are you going?
Janet:	I'm going to the library. Can you take me?
Taxi driver:	Yes, of course, no problem. Do you come from Swansea?
Janet:	No, I come from Vermont.

Gyrrwr tacsi: Vermont? Jiw, jiw! Mae Dad yn dod o Efrog Newydd! A, dyma ni, wrth y llyfrgell. Tair punt, os gwelwch yn dda.

Janet: Dyma bum punt. Cadwch y newid.

Yn y llyfrgell:

Janet: Esgusodwch fi, ydych chi'n gwybod ble mae llyfrau ar achau'r teulu?

Llyfrgellydd: Ydw. Maen nhw ar y silff ar y dde.

Taxi driver: Vermont? Dear me! Dad comes from New York! Ah, here we are, by the library. Three pounds, please.

Janet: Here are five pounds. Keep the change.

In the library:

Janet: Excuse me. Do you know where the books on family trees are?

Librarian: They are on the shelf on the right.

Ymadroddion a Geirfa / Phrases and Vocabulary

Esgusodwch fi.	Excuse me.
Ble mae … ?	Where is … ?
Ble mae'r … ?	Where is the … ?
ewch	go
i'r chwith	to the left
i'r dde	to the right
chwilio am	(to) look for
yn syth ymlaen	straight ahead
Ydw i?	Am I?
Ydych.	Yes (you are).
ddim	not
Diolch yn fawr.	Thank you very much.

Gramadeg / Grammar

Asking and answering questions

Form of verb 'to be'	Subject	yn (or 'n)	Verb	Object	Answer
Ydw	i	'n	dal	tacsi?	Ydych.

Ydw i 'n dal tacsi?
Do I take a taxi? — Ydych. Yes (you do).

Wyt ti 'n dal bws?
Are you taking a bus? — Ydw. Yes (I am).

Ydy e 'n dal trên?
Is he catching a train? — Ydy. Yes (he is).

Ydy hi 'n mynd â beic?
Is she taking a bike? — Ydy. Yes (she is).

Ydyn ni 'n gwybod y ffordd?
Do we know the way? — Ydyn. Yes (we do).

Ydych chi 'n gwybod y ffordd?
Do you know the way? — Ydw. Yes (I do).

Ydyn nhw 'n gwerthu map?
Do they sell a map? — Ydyn. Yes (they do).

Alternative form, often heard (*pronunciations in italics*)

Ydych chi?	→	Y'ch chi?
uhdich chee		*eech chee*

Ydyn ni?	→	Y'n ni?
uhdin nee		*een nee*

Answer no

Na	*or*	nag ydw	I'm not
		nag wyt	you're not
		nag yw	he, she isn't
		nag ydyn	we're not *or* no, they're not
		nag ydych	you're not

GEIRFA YCHWANEGOL / ADDITIONAL VOCABULARY

chwilio am	(to) look for
ar goll	lost
esgusodwch fi	excuse me
gwybod	(to) know
yn bell	far
stryd	street
fawr	big, high
wrth gwrs	of course
ewch	go
gwesty	hotel
y gylchfan	the roundabout
wrth	by
ar hyd	along
diolch yn fawr i chi	thank you very much
codi	(to) raise
llaw	hand
gallu	(to) be able (to)
problem	problem
jiw jiw!	dear me!

dyma ni	here we are
tair	three
punt	pound
cadwch	keep
newid	(to) change
os gwelwch yn dda	please
dyma bum punt	here's five pounds (£5)
silff	shelf
tacsi	taxi

Y MARFERION/ EXERCISES

1. Read the Welsh aloud several times.

2. Cover the English side. Translate the Welsh. Check after each sentence, then attempt it all. Do this several times.

3. Cover the Welsh side. Translate the English. Check after each sentence, then attempt it all. Do this several times.

   NOTE: DO THE ABOVE THREE EXERCISES WITH ALL THE LESSONS TO COME. THESE INSTRUCTIONS WILL NOT BE REPEATED.

4. Make up as many sensible questions as you can, selecting words from each column:

   For example:
   Ydych chi'n gwybod ble mae'r llyfrgell?
   Do you know where the library is?

Ydych chi'n Do you know … **Ydy'r tacsi'n** Is the taxi going to …	**gwybod** **mynd**	**ble mae'r** **i'r**	**llyfrgell** sinema theatr gwesty

5. Answer yes to the above questions.

6. Translate:

Go to the left.
Go to the right.
Go straight ahead.
Go to the high street.
Go to the cinema.
Go to the library.
Go to the hotel.

7. Janet is in the circle marked X. Tell her how she can get to the places mentioned.

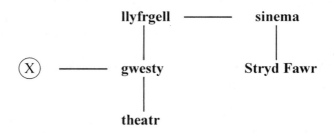

For example:
Ewch yn syth ymlaen i'r gwesty.
Wrth y gwesty ewch i'r chwith i'r llyfrgell.

Extra Grammar

1. The article in Welsh:

There is no word for 'a' or 'an'. It is simply left out, so **theatr** means 'theater' or 'a theater'.

'The' is usually **y**:

y theatr	the theater
y sinema	the cinema
y stryd	the street

Before vowels, **y** becomes **yr**:

yr ysgo	the school
yr afon	the river
yr afal	the apple

After vowels, **y** and **yr** become **'r**:

Mae'r theatr yn y	The theater is in the
stryd fawr.	high street.
i'r gwesty	to the hotel

2. Translating present tense verbs:

Ydych chi can mean 'do you' or 'are you' according to context:

Ydych chi'n dod?	Are you coming?
Ydych chi'n hoffi coffi?	Do you like coffee?

Forms of the present tense can also be translated with or without using the verb 'to be' in English:

Rwy'n cerdded.	I walk *or* I am walking.

GWERS CHWECH
LESSON SIX

DEIALOG: BETH SY'N DIGWYDD?

Mae Janet yn y llyfrgell. Mae hi'n gofyn beth sy yn Abertawe heno. Mae hi'n moyn mynd i'r theatr neu i'r sinema.

Janet:	Diolch yn fawr am eich help.
Llyfgrellydd:	Croeso.
Janet:	Wel, rwy'n chwilio am wybodaeth am heno. Rwy'n moyn mynd i'r sinema, neu i'r theatr. Oes theatr yn Abertawe?
Llyfrgellydd:	Oes, mae tair theatr yma. Theatr y Grand yw'r theatr fwyaf. Mae Theatr Dylan Thomas wrth y Marina, ac mae Theatr Taliesin yn y coleg.
Janet:	Ydych chi'n gwybod beth sy yn y theatrau heno?
Llyfrgellydd:	Na, dw i ddim yn gwybod, ond mae'r papur lleol gyda fi. Un funud. A, dyma fe. Mae drama gan Alan Ayckbourn yn y Grand ac mae ffilm yn Theatr Taliesin. Ydych chi'n hoffi Alan Ayckbourn?
Janet:	Na, dw i ddim yn hoffi Ayckbourn. Pa ffilm sy yn y theatr?
Llyfrgellydd:	Dw i ddim yn siŵr. Ffilm o Rwsia, rwy'n credu, Rhyfel a Heddwch. Ydych chi'n hoffi'r nofel?
Janet:	Na, dw i ddim yn hoffi'r nofel—mae'n hir iawn. Oes sinema yn Abertawe?
Llyfrgellydd:	Oes, wrth gwrs. Mae dwy sinema yma, ac mae sawl sgrîn yn y ddwy sinema.
Janet:	Oes ffilmiau da yn y sinemâu?
Llyfrgellydd:	Na, does dim llawer o ffilmiau da yma. O, un funud, mae ffilm dda yn yr Odeon: ffilm James Bond.
Janet:	Dw i ddim yn hoffi James Bond! Oes cyngerdd yn Abertawe heno?

DIALOGUE: WHAT'S ON?

Janet is in the library. She is asking what is (on) in Swansea tonight. She wants to go to the theater or to the cinema.

Janet: Thank you for your help.

Librarian: Not at all.

Janet: Well, I'm looking for information for tonight. I want to go to the cinema, or to the theater. Is there a theater in Swansea?

Librarian: Yes, there are three theaters here. The Grand Theater is the biggest theater. Dylan Thomas Theater is by the Marina, and Taliesin Theater is in the college.

Janet: Do you know what is in the theaters tonight?

Librarian: No, I don't know, but I have the local paper. One moment. Ah, here it is. There is a play by Alan Ayckbourn in the Grand, and there's a film in Taliesin Theater. Do you like Alan Ayckbourn?

Janet: No, I don't like Ayckbourn. Which film is in the theater?

Librarian: I'm not sure. A film from Russia, I believe, *War and Peace*. Do you like the novel?

Janet: No, I don't like the novel—it's very long. Is there a cinema in Swansea?

Librarian: Yes, of course. There are two cinemas here, and there are several screens in the two cinemas.

Janet: Are there good films at the cinemas?

Librarian: No, there aren't many good films here. Oh, one moment, there is a good film at the Odeon: a James Bond film.

Janet: I don't like James Bond! Is there a concert in Swansea tonight?

Llyfrgellydd: Oes, mae cyngerdd yn Neuadd y Brangwyn.
                 Nawfed symffoni Beethoven.
Janet: Hyfryd! O'r diwedd. Ydw i'n gallu cael tocynnau
                 dros y ffôn?
Llyfrgellydd: Dw i ddim yn siŵr. Dyma'r ffôn.

Mae Janet yn ffonio.

Janet: Prynhawn da ... rydw i'n moyn un tocyn i'r
                 cyngerdd heno ... Deg punt? Na, dw i ddim yn
                 moyn talu deg punt ... Wyth punt? Iawn ... Un
                 tocyn wyth punt, os gwelwch chi'n dda.

Librarian: Yes, there is a concert in the Brangwyn Hall. Beethoven's Ninth Symphony.

Janet: Lovely! At last. Can I get tickets over the phone?

Librarian: I'm not sure. Here's the phone.

Janet phones.

Janet: Good afternoon … I want one ticket for the concert tonight … Ten pounds? No, I don't want to pay ten pounds … Eight pounds? Fine … One ticket for eight pounds, please.

YMADRODDION A GEIRFA / PHRASES AND VOCABULARY

Beth sy yn y theatr?	What's in the theater?
y dafarn	the pub
y ganolfan hamdden	the leisure center
yr eglwys	the church
y neuadd	the hall
neuadd y dref	the town hall
ysgol	school
coleg	college
prifysgol	university
wn i ddim	I don't know
ffilm	film
drama	drama
cyngerdd	concert
arddangosfa	exhibition
nofio	swimming
hoffi	(to) like

GRAMADEG / GRAMMAR

The negative sentence

Negative of verb 'to be'	Subject	Negative + yn	Verb	Object
Dw	i	ddim yn	hoffi	drama.

I don't like drama.

Dwyt	ti	ddim yn	hoffi	ffilmiau.

You don't like films.

Dyw	e	ddim yn	hoffi	cyngerdd.

He doesn't like a concert.

Dyw	hi	ddim yn	hoffi	nofio.

She doesn't like swimming.

Dyw	Sian	ddim yn	hoffi	yfed.

Sian doesn't like drinking.

Dyw'r	plant	ddim yn	hoffi	chwarae.

The children don't like playing.

Dy'n	ni	ddim yn	hoffi	drama.

We don't like drama.

Dy'ch	chi	ddim yn	hoffi	cerdded.

You don't like walking.

Dy'n	nhw	ddim yn	hoffi	dal bws.

They don't like to catch a bus.

Alternative forms and pronunciations
(*pronunciations in italics*)

Dw i ddim	→	**Dydw i ddim**
doo ee thim		*duhdoo ee thim*

Dyw e ddim	→	**Dydy e ddim**
dioo eh thim		*duhdee eh thim*

Dyw hi ddim	→	**Dydy hi ddim**
dioo hee thim		*duhdee hee thim*

Dy'n ni ddim	→	**Dydyn ni ddim**
deen nee thim		*duhdin nee thim*

Dy'ch chi ddim	→	**Dydych chi ddim**
deech chee thim		*duhdich chee thim*

Dy'n nhw ddim	→	**Dydyn nhw ddim**
deen nhoo thim		*duhdin nhoo thim*

GEIRFA YCHWANEGOL / ADDITIONAL VOCABULARY

beth sy	what is
heno	tonight
neu	or
am	for
croeso	welcome, not at all
gofynnwch am wybodaeth	ask for information
am heno	about tonight
oes? oes	is there? yes
tair	three [with feminine nouns]
fwyaf	biggest
coleg	college
theatrau	theaters
papur	paper
lleol	local
un funud	one minute, one moment
dyma fe	here it is
gan	by
does dim	there isn't
dim byd	nothing
with punt	eight pounds (£8)
hoff	fond
hyfryd	pleasant, lovely
iawn	very
pa	which
o Rwsia	from Russia
rhyfel	war
heddwch	peace
nofel	novel
hir	long
dwy	two
sawl	several [followed by singular noun]
sgrîn	screen
ffilmiau	films
dda	good
siŵr	sure
cyngerdd	concert

nawfed	ninth
symffoni	symphony
un	one
o'r diwedd	at last
tocyn	ticket
tocynnau	tickets
dros y ffôn	over the phone
deg punt	ten pounds (£10)
talu	(to) pay

YMARFERION / EXERCISES

1. Make as many sentences as possible, selecting words from each column:

Dydw i	ddim yn	hoffi	ffilmiau
Dyw hi			dramâu
Dy'n ni			nofelau
Dy'ch chi			cyngherddau

2. Translate the following:

   Rwy'n hoffi'r nofel, ond dw i ddim yn hoffi'r ffilm.
   Rwy'n hoffi cerdded, ond dw i ddim yn hoffi nofio.
   Rwy'n hoffi coffi, ond dw i ddim yn hoffi te.
   Rwy'n hoffi Beethoven, ond dw i ddim yn hoffi Mozart.

3. Make up similar sentences to those in Exercise 2 above, using the following words:

Schubert	**Brahms**
nofelau	**dramâu**
Vermont	**Abertawe**
ffilmiau James Bond	**ffilmiau Spielberg**
dal bws	**cerdded**

Extra Grammar

1. There is / There are:

   Mae on its own means 'there is' or 'there are':
   Mae drama yn y theatr.   There's a drama at the theater.

   Oes? asks the question 'is there?' or 'are there?':
   Oes ffilm yn y sinema?   Is there a film at the cinema?

   The answer 'yes' is **oes**:
   Oes, mae ffilm yn y sinema. Yes, there is a film at the cinema.

   The answer 'no' is **na** or **nag oes**:
   Na, does dim ffilm yno.   No, there's no film there.

2. Emphasis:
   To emphasize a noun, put it at the start of the sentence, and use **sy** for 'is':
   Ayckbourn sy yn y theatr.   It's Ayckbourn who's in the theater.

3. Numbers:
   Numbers are followed by singular nouns:
   un caffe   **pum punt**   **wyth potel**

4. Plurals:
   Many Welsh words form their plural by adding **-au** or **-iau**:

nofel	**nofelau**	**theatr**	**theatrau**
cyngerdd	**cyngherddau**	**ffilm**	**ffilmiau**

   Note these two:

drama	**dramâu**	**sinema**	**sinemâu**

GWERS SAITH

LESSON SEVEN

DEIALOG: AROS NOSON

Mae Janet yn cyrraedd gwesty.

Janet: Noswaith dda.

Mr. Jones: Noswaith dda. Ga i helpu?

Janet: Rydw i'n chwilio am lety.

Mr. Jones: Am sawl noson?

Janet: Am saith noson.

Mr. Jones: Ystafell sengl neu ddwbl?

Janet: Wi'n chwilio am ystafell sengl. Oes ystafell sengl 'da chi?

Mr. Jones: Oes, ac mae tŷ bach a chawod yn yr ystafell wely.

Janet: Da iawn. Beth yw cost yr ystafell?

Mr. Jones: Pymtheg punt y nos.

Janet: Ydy'r pris yn cynnwys brecwast?

Mr. Jones: Ydy. Mae brecwast Cymreig llawn yma.

Janet: Diolch. Ga i'r ystafell am wythnos?

Mr. Jones: Croeso. Oes cesys 'da chi?

Janet: Oes, mae un ces 'da fi.

Mr. Jones: Ga i helpu?

Janet: Croeso, diolch. Oes bar 'da chi?

Mr. Jones: Oes, mae bar 'da ni, ac mae ystafell fwyta 'da ni—ryn ni'n gwneud cinio yn y dydd a swper yn y nos.

Janet: Ble dw i'n gallu gadael y car?

Mr. Jones: Ar y stryd yn y dydd, ond mae lle parcio 'da ni, yn y cefn. Unrhyw beth arall?

Janet: Ga i'r allwedd i'r ystafell, os gwelwch yn dda?

Mr. Jones: Wrth gwrs. Dyma fe.

Janet: Ydy'r bar ar agor?

DIALOGUE: STAYING THE NIGHT

Janet arrives at a hotel.

Janet: Good evening.

Mr. Jones: Good evening. May I help?

Janet: I'm looking for lodgings.

Mr. Jones: For how many nights?

Janet: For seven nights.

Mr. Jones: Single room or a double?

Janet: I'm looking for a single room. Have you got a single room?

Mr. Jones: Yes, and there is a toilet and a shower in the bedroom.

Janet: Very good. What is the cost of the room?

Mr. Jones: Fifteen pounds a night.

Janet: Does the price include breakfast?

Mr. Jones: Yes. There is a full Welsh breakfast here.

Janet: Thanks. May I have the room for a week?

Mr. Jones: Welcome. Have you got suitcases?

Janet: Yes, I have one suitcase.

Mr. Jones: May I help?

Janet: Welcome, thanks. Have you got a bar?

Mr. Jones: Yes, we have a bar, and we have a dining room—we make lunch in the day and supper in the evening.

Janet: Where can I leave the car?

Mr. Jones: On the street in the day, but we have a parking space, in the back. Anything else?

Janet: May I have the key to the room, please?

Mr. Jones: Of course. Here it is.

Janet: Is the bar open?

Ymadroddion a Geirfa / Phrases and Vocabulary

gwesty	hotel
gwely	bed
llety	lodgings
chwilio am	(to) look for
un noson	one night
wythnos	week
gwely a brecwast	bed and breakfast
cinio	dinner, lunch
aros am	(to) stay for
swper	supper
diod	drink
ystafell	room
ystafell ymolchi	bathroom
tŷ bach	toilet
papur tŷ bach	toilet paper
sebon	soap
tywel	towel
cawod	shower
dillad gwely	bedclothes
bwyta	(to) eat
cadw lle	(to) book a room
yfed	(to) drink
cês	case
lle parcio	parking space

GRAMADEG / GRAMMAR

'I have' (possess) or 'I have got' is translated using the preposition **gyda**:

Mae car gyda fi.   I have a car.   (lit. 'There is a car with me.')

Gyda is often shortened to **'da**.

Mae	car	'da	fi	car
	cawod		ti	shower
	ystafell wely		fe	bedroom
	cês		hi	case
	lle parcio		ni	parking space
Oes	bwyd da		chi	good food
	bar		nhw	bar

To ask if someone has something, change the **mae** to **oes**:

Oes bar 'da chi?   Have you got a bar?
  Oes.   Yes.
  Na.   No.

GEIRFA YCHWANEGOL / ADDITIONAL VOCABULARY

sawl	how many
noson	night
sengl	single
dwbl, ddwbl	double
cost	cost
pris	price
cynnwys	(to) include
Cymreig	Welsh
llawn	full
cesys	cases
ystafell fwyta	dining room

ystafell wely	bedroom
bar	bar
yn y dydd	during the day
yn y cefn	in the back
unrhyw	any
unrhyw beth	anything
arall	else, other
allwedd	key
croeso	welcome
dyma	here is
dyma fe	here it is

YMARFERION / EXERCISES

1. Say that you have the following things:

    For example:
    bag   **Mae bag 'da fi.**   I have a bag.

    car   llety   ystafell sengl   gwely dwbl   lle parcio

2. Answer the following questions:

    a) **Oes car 'da chi?**
    b) **Oes cawod 'da chi yn yr ystafell wely?**
    c) **Oes gwely dwbl 'da chi?**
    d) **Oes gwely sengl 'da chi?**

3. Translate the following:

    I am looking for a single room.
    For how many nights?
    For one night.
    May I have a double room?
    Has it got a toilet?
    Yes, and a shower.
    May I have the room, please?

Extra Grammar

Other phrases using **'da**:

I have a headache.	**Mae pen tost 'da fi.**
I have a cold.	**Mae annwyd 'da fi.**
I'd rather go.	**Mae'n well 'da fi fynd.**
I'd rather have an orange.	**Mae'n well 'da fi oren.**

GWERS WYTH

LESSON EIGHT

DEIALOG: YN Y BAR

Mae Janet yn y bar yn y gwesty. Mae hi'n edrych ar y prisiau.

Janet: Peint o gwrw, un bunt saith deg ceiniog; gwydraid o
          win gwyn, un bunt chwe deg ceiniog; sieri, un bunt
          pedwar deg ceiniog; jin a tonic, un bunt chwe deg
          ceiniog; peint o Guinness, dwy bunt; ...
Barman: Ga i helpu? Beth ydych chi'n moyn?
Janet: Sudd lemwn, efallai, sudd oren, sudd afal. Mae
          gormod o ddewis yma. Dŵr efallai. Oes dŵr o Gymru
          'da chi?
Barman: Oes, mae dŵr Tŷ Nant 'da ni. Ydych chi'n moyn potel
          o ddŵr?
Janet: Dw i ddim yn siŵr. Faint yw'r gwin coch?
Barman: Un bunt, chwe deg ceiniog.
Janet: Faint yw hanner peint o gwrw?
Barman: Naw deg ceiniog.
Janet: A faint yw seidir?
Barman: Dwy bunt y peint, neu hanner peint am bunt.
Janet: Pa fath o gwrw sy 'da chi?
Barman: Cwrw melyn, cwrw mwyn, cwrw tywyll ...
Janet: Hanner peint o gwrw mwyn, os gwelwch yn dda, gyda
          thipyn bach o lemwnêd.
Barman: Naw deg ceiniog, os gwelwch yn dda.
Janet: Dyma bunt.
Barman: A dyma ddeg ceiniog o newid. Iechyd da i chi!
Janet: Iechyd da! Ydych chi'n gwerthu bwyd?
Barman: Ydyn. Ryn ni'n gwerthu creision, cnau, a rholiau.
          Rholiau ham a salad, ffowlyn, caws a salad.
Janet: Ydych chi'n gwneud bwyd twym?
Barman: Ydyn. Cyw yn y fasged, pysgod a sglodion, lasagne a
          salad.

DIALOGUE: IN THE BAR

Janet is in the bar in the hotel. She's looking at the prices.

Janet: A pint of beer, £1.70p; a glass of white wine, £1.60p; sherry, £1.40p; gin and tonic, £1.60p; a pint of Guinness, £2; ...

Barman: May I help? What do you want?

Janet: Lemon juice, perhaps, orange juice, apple juice. There is too much choice here. Water, perhaps. Have you got water from Wales?

Barman: Yes, we have Tŷ Nant water. Do you want a bottle of water?

Janet: I'm not sure. How much is the red wine?

Barman: £1.60p.

Janet: How much is half a pint of beer?

Barman: 90p.

Janet: And how much is cider?

Barman: £2 a pint, or half a pint for a £1.

Janet: What kind of beer do you have?

Barman: Bitter beer, mild beer, dark beer ...

Janet: Half a pint of mild beer, please, with a little lemonade.

Barman: 90p, please.

Janet: Here is a pound.

Barman: And here is 10p change. Good health to you!

Janet: Good health! Do you sell food?

Barman: Yes. We sell crisps, nuts, and rolls. Ham and salad rolls, chicken, cheese, and salad.

Janet: Do you do hot food?

Barman: Yes. Chicken in the basket, fish and chips, lasagna, and salad.

Janet: Faint yw'r bwyd?

Barman: Tair punt pum deg am fwyd twym. Punt pum deg yw'r rholiau.

Janet: Cyw yn y fasged os gwelwch yn dda. Dyma bum punt.

Barman: Un bunt pum deg o newid.

Janet: How much is the food?
Barman: £3.50 for hot food. The rolls are £1.50.

Janet: Chicken in the basket, please. Here are five pounds.
Barman: £1.50 change.

Ymadroddion a Geirfa / Phrases and Vocabulary

peint	pint
cwrw	beer
gwin	wine
gwydraid o	a glass of
gwin gwyn	white wine
gwin coch	red wine
hanner peint	half a pint
cadair	chair
jin	gin
tonic	tonic
sieri	sherry
iâ	ice
dŵr	water
potel	bottle

Gramadeg / Grammar

Masculine and feminine nouns

All nouns in Welsh are either masculine or feminine. For example:

Masculine		Feminine	
dyn	man	menyw	woman
bachgen	boy	merch	girl
tad	father	mam	mother
tad-cu	grandfather	mam-gu	grandmother
brawd	brother	chwaer	sister
cefnder	cousin	cyfnither	cousin
tŷ	house	gardd	garden
car	car	ffenestr	window
teledu	television	stryd	street
pentref	village	tref	town
bwrdd	table	desg	desk
parc	park	dinas	city
llyfr	book	ffilm	film

trên	train	**llong**	ship
tocyn	ticket	**gorsaf**	station
gwesty	hotel	**ystafell**	room

The first letter of feminine nouns can change ('mutate') after the definite article ('the') – **y**, **yr** or **'r**. This change is called 'soft mutation'. The following are the letters that can change:

c > **g**	**cath**	(cat)	**y gath**
p > **p**	**pont**	(bridge)	**y bont**
t > **d**	**tref**	(town)	**y dref**
g > **/**	**gardd**	(garden)	**yr ardd** (the 'g' disappears)
b > **f**	**basged**	(basket)	**y fasged**
d > **dd**	**dinas**	(city)	**y dd**inas
m > **f**	**mam**	(mother)	**y fam**

Two other letters can also change in other circumstances (to be discussed at the end of this lesson):

ll > **l**   **rh** > **r**

Geirfa Ychwanegol / Additional Vocabulary

sudd (m)	juice
lemwn (m)	lemon
oren (m)	orange
afal (m/f)	apple
dŵr (m)	water
Cymru (f)	Wales
potel (f)	bottle
hanner (m)	half
hanner peint	half a pint
cwrw (m)	beer
melyn	yellow
mwyn	mild
tywyll	dark
newid	change
tipyn bach o	a little (of)

Iechyd da!	Good health! Cheers!
gwerthu	(to) sell
bwyd (m)	food
creision (pl)	crisps
rholiau (pl)	rolls
ham (m)	ham
salad (m)	salad
ffowlyn (m)	chicken
caws (m)	cheese
twym	warm
basged (f)	basket

Ymarferion / Exercises

1. Say you would like:

a glass of wine	half a pint of beer
a bottle of water	a pint of cider
a glass of white wine	apple juice
orange juice	a glass or red wine
half a pint of Guinness	

   Examples:
   Rwy'n moyn peint o gwrw, os gwelwch yn dda.
   or
   Ga i beint o gwrw, os gwelwch yn dda?

2. Give the following prices:

£5	£2.50	£3.50	£7.00
£10	£1.50	£8.00	£9.00

Extra Grammar

Soft Mutations

The letter changes mentioned above occur often. They change in the following circumstances:

1. After **y**, **yr** and **'r** (the).
2. After **dau** (m), **dwy** (f) (two).
3. After **o** (of).
4. After **am** (for, at).
5. After **dyma** (here is, here are).
6. Feminine nouns after **un** (one).
7. After **ga i** (may I have).

GWERS NAW

LESSON NINE

Deialog: Amser Brecwast

Mae Janet yn codi am saith o'r gloch, ac mae hi'n cael brecwast yn y gwesty.

Gweinydd:	Bore da! Ydych chi'n barod i gael brecwast?
Janet:	Bore da! Beth sy i frecwast?
Gweinydd:	Mae digon o ddewis. Ydych chi'n moyn brecwast oer neu dwym?
Janet:	Brecwast twym, os gwelwch yn dda.
Gweinydd:	Wel, mae 'da ni wy, cig moch, selsig, tomatos, tost.
Janet:	Wy wedi'i ffrio, os gwelwch yn dda, cig moch, tost bara brown a mêl, ond dim selsig, a dim tomatos—a digon o halen.
Gweinydd:	Ydych chi'n moyn te neu goffi?
Janet:	Coffi du, os gwelwch yn dda... Mae'r plât yma'n frwnt.
Gweinydd:	O, mae'n flin 'da fi. Wi'n mynd i nôl plât arall.
Janet:	Ac mae'r fforc yma'n frwnt hefyd.
Gweinydd:	Wi'n mynd i nôl fforc lân nawr.
Janet:	Diolch! Oes papur newyddion 'da chi?
Gweinydd:	Oes, dyma fe.
Janet:	Does dim llwy de 'da fi.
Gweinydd:	Mae'n flin 'da fi. Dyma lwy de i chi.
Janet:	Oes llaeth 'da chi?
Gweinydd:	Oes, mae llaeth yn y jwg glas, ac mae Corn Flakes yn y fowlen binc ar y bwrdd.
Janet:	Hyfryd, diolch yn fawr.
Gweinydd:	Unrhyw beth arall?
Janet:	Y bil, os gwelwch yn dda.
Gweinydd:	Does dim bil—rydych chi'n talu am wely a brecwast.

DIALOGUE: BREAKFAST TIME

Janet gets up at seven o'clock, and she's having breakfast in the hotel.

Waiter: Good morning! Are you ready to have breakfast?

Janet: Good morning! What's for breakfast?

Waiter: There's plenty of choice. Do you want a cold or warm breakfast?

Janet: A warm breakfast, please.

Waiter: Well, we have egg, bacon, sausages, tomatoes, toast.

Janet: A fried egg, please. Bacon, brown-bread toast and honey, but no sausages, and no tomatoes—and plenty of salt.

Waiter: Do you want tea or coffee?

Janet: Black coffee, please... This plate is dirty.

Waiter: Oh, I'm sorry. I'm going to get another plate.

Janet: And this fork is dirty too.

Waiter: I'm going to get a clean fork now.

Janet: Thanks! Do you have a newspaper?

Waiter: Yes, here it is.

Janet: I haven't got a teaspoon.

Waiter: I'm sorry. Here's a teaspoon for you.

Janet: Have you got milk?

Waiter: Yes, there's milk in the blue jug, and there are Corn Flakes in the pink bowl on the table.

Janet: Lovely, thanks.

Waiter: Anything else?

Janet: The bill, please.

Waiter: There's no bill—you're paying for bed and breakfast.

YMADRODDION A GEIRFA / PHRASES AND VOCABULARY

bara (m)	bread
tost (m)	toast
coffi (m)	coffee
te (m)	tea
mêl (m)	honey
jam (m)	jam
tebot (m)	teapot
llaeth (m)	milk
siwgr (m)	sugar
wy (m)	egg
halen (m)	salt
pupur (m)	pepper
jwg (m)	jug
llwy de	teaspoon
marmalêd (m)	marmalade
cig moch (m)	bacon
soser (f)	saucer
cwpan (m/f)	cup
cwpaned o de	a cup of tea
cwpaned o goffi	a cup of coffee
plât (m)	plate
fforc (f)	ffork
cyllell (f)	knife
llwy (f)	spoon
wy wedi'i ferwi	boiled egg
wy wedi'i ffrio	fried egg
selsig (f)	sausages
tomato (m)	tomato

Gramadeg / Grammar

Adjectives

Adjectives in Welsh usually follow the noun:

brecwast mawr   big breakfast

Adjectives mutate after feminine nouns:

llwy fawr   a big spoon

Adjectives mutate after **yn** as part of the verb 'be':

Mae'r brecwast yn fawr.   The breakfast is big.

Hen (old) is used before the noun, and the noun is mutated:

Hen dŷ   old house

Adverbs

To form adverbs, simply put **yn** before the adjective and mutate:

da   good   →   **yn dda**   well

Lliwiau / Colors

gwyn	white
coch	red
melyn	yellow
glas	blue
gwyrdd	green
porffor	purple
aur	gold
arian	silver
du	black
brown	brown

llwyd	grey
oren	orange
pinc	pink
golau	light
tywyll	dark

GEIRFA YCHWANEGOL / ADDITIONAL VOCABULARY

cael	have, get
brecwast (m)	breakfast
i frecwast	for breakfast
oer	cold
twym	warm, hot
brwnt	dirty
mae'n flin'da fi	I'm sorry
bowlen (f)	bowl
hyfryd	lovely, pleasant
bil (m)	bill
talu	(to) pay
gwely (m)	bed
glân	clean
papur newyddion (m)	newspaper

YMARFERION / EXERCISES

1. Translate:

What's for breakfast?
May I have a cup of black coffee?
I want brown bread, please.
Have you got any milk?
May I have bacon, toast and egg?

2. Link words in the left column to adjectives in the right:

gwin	**glân**
brecwast	**gwyn**
bara	**twym**
plât	**brown**

3. Mutate the following adjectives after the feminine nouns:

llwy + glân
ffilm + da
fforc + brwnt

Extra Grammar

Comparison of adjectives

1. Long form:

as ... as	**mor ... â**	
	mor lân â	as clean as
		(note soft mutation after **mor**)
more	**mwy**; than **na**	
	mwy glân na	cleaner than
most	**mwya**	
	mwya glân	most clean

2. Short form:

...er ...**ach**		
	glanach na	cleaner than
...est ...**af**		
	glanaf	cleanest

GWERS DEG

LESSON TEN

DEIALOG: CAEL CINIO

Mae Janet a Mari ei ffrind wedi mynd i'r tŷ bwyta i gael cinio.
Maen nhw wedi eistedd wrth y bwrdd, ac maen nhw'n edrych ar
y fwydlen.

Janet:	Wel, Mari, beth wyt ti eisiau cael i ginio?
Mari:	Rwy wedi bwyta gormod i frecwast, ac ry'n ni wedi cael coffi. Dw i ddim eisiau bwyta llawer.
Janet:	Ond mae rhaid i ti gael rhywbeth.
Mari:	O'r gorau. Fe ga i bysgodyn.
Gweinydd:	Ydych chi wedi dewis eto?
Janet:	Na, dw i ddim wedi dewis eto.
Gweinydd:	Ydych chi am gael rhywbeth i yfed?
Janet:	Gwin coch os gwelwch yn dda. Wyt ti wedi dewis, Mari?
Mari:	Wi eisiau cael sudd oren.
Gweinydd:	Beth hoffech chi gael i ddechrau?
Janet:	Dim byd i ddechrau. Ry'n ni wedi bwyta gormod i frecwast. Ond hoffwn i gael cyw a llysiau.
Gweinydd:	Cyw wedi'i rostio?
Janet:	Ie, os gwelwch yn dda.
Gweinydd:	Tatws wedi berwi?
Janet:	Na, sglodion, os gwelwch yn dda.
Gweinydd:	Pwdin?
Janet:	Hufen iâ a ffrwythau.
Gweinydd:	A chithau?
Mari:	Eog mewn saws gwyn, os gwelwch yn dda, a thatws newydd.
Gweinydd:	Ac i bwdin?
Mari:	Tarten afalau, os gwelwch yn dda.
Janet:	O daro, ry'n ni'n mynd i fwyta gormod, unwaith eto.

DIALOGUE: HAVING LUNCH (DINNER)

Janet and her friend have gone into a restaurant to have lunch. They have sat at the table, and they are looking at the menu.

Janet: Well, Mari, what do you want for lunch?

Mari: I have eaten too much for breakfast, and we have had coffee. I don't want to eat a lot.

Janet: But you must have something.

Mari: All right. I shall have fish.

Waiter: Have you chosen yet?

Janet: No, I haven't chosen yet.

Waiter: Do you want to have something to drink?

Janet: Red wine, please. Have you chosen, Mari?

Mari: I want to have orange juice.

Waiter: What would you like to start?

Janet: Nothing to start. We have eaten too much for breakfast. But I would like to have chicken and vegetables.

Waiter: Roasted chicken?

Janet: Yes, please.

Waiter: Boiled potatoes?

Janet: No. Chips, please.

Waiter: Sweet?

Janet: Ice cream and fruit.

Waiter: And you?

Mari: Salmon in white sauce, please, and new potatoes.

Waiter: And for sweet?

Mari: Apple pie, please.

Janet: Oh dear, we are going to eat too much, once again.

Ymadroddion a Geirfa / Phrases and Vocabulary

caffe (m)	café
tŷ bwyta (m)	restaurant
bwydlen (f)	menu
cig (m)	meat
eidion (m)	beef
oen (m)	lamb
cyw (m)	chicken
ffowlyn (m)	chicken
porc (m)	pork
llysiau (pl)	vegetables
tatws (pl)	potatoes
sglodion (pl)	chips
bresych (pl)	cabbage
moron (pl)	carrots
pys (pl)	peas
letys (pl)	lettuce
pysgod (pl)	fish
eog (m)	salmon
penfras (m)	cod
brithyll (m)	trout
lleden (f)	plaice (a flat fish)
sewin (m)	sewin (river salmon)
caws (m)	cheese
menyn (m)	butter
ffrwythau (pl)	fruit
afalau (pl)	apples
orennau (pl)	oranges
gellyg (pl)	pears
grawnwin (pl)	grapes
banana (m)	banana
eirin (pl)	plums
eirin gwlanog (pl)	peaches
pwdin (m)	sweet, pudding
cwstard (m)	custard
reis (m)	rice
hufen iâ (m)	ice cream
tarten (f)	tart, pie

GRAMADEG / GRAMMAR

Past tense: Saying you have done something

This is much easier in Welsh than in English. Simply replace the **yn** or **'n** used with the present tense with **wedi**:

- yn -	- wedi -
Mae e'n mynd.	**Mae e wedi mynd.**
He is going.	He has gone.
Rwy'n yfed.	**Rwy wedi yfed.**
I am drinking.	I have drunk.
Ydy e'n dod?	**Ydy e wedi dod?**
Is he coming?	Has he come?
Ydy hi'n bwyta?	**Ydy hi wedi bwyta?**
Is she eating?	Has she eaten?

In English, the verb has to change: eat > eaten; drink > drunk. This does not happen in Welsh:

Dyw e ddim wedi cyrraedd.	He hasn't arrived.
Maen nhw wedi gorffen.	They have finished.
Dy'n ni ddim wedi codi.	We haven't got up.
Ry'ch chi wedi mwynhau.	You have enjoyed.

GEIRFA YCHWANEGOL / VOCABULARY

i ginio	for dinner
i frecwast	for breakfast
i de	for tea
eisiau	want
rhywbeth	something
fe	[no meaning; it confirms the verb]
fe ga i	I'll have
dewis	choose
eto	yet, again

unwaith eto	once again
hoffech	you would like, would you like?
dim byd	nothing
hoffwn	I would like
dechrau	start
rhostio	(to) roast
berwi	(to) boil
chithau	you (with emphasis)
saws (m)	sauce
newydd	new
daro	dear

YMARFERION / EXERCISES

1. Make up sentences taking words from each column:

Rwy Mae hi	wedi	bwyta yfed	tost te cyw sglodion wy wedi'i ffrio selsig	i frecwast i ginio

2. Say what you have had today, for breakfast and for lunch.

For example:
I frecwast, rwy wedi bwyta tost a jam. Rwy wedi yfed coffi.

Extra Grammar

1. Would like:

    Note how the verb **hoffi** can be used to mean 'would like':

hoffwn i	I would like
hoffet ti	you would like
hoffai fe	he would like
hoffai hi	she would like
hoffen ni	we would like
hoffech chi	you would like
hoffen nhw	they would like
hoffech chi?	would you like?
hoffwn	yes (I would like)

    All these are followed by *soft mutation*:

Hoffwn i fynd.	I would like to go.

2. Another mutation: aspirate mutation after **a**:

    The following changes occur to the first letters of nouns after **a** (and) and also after **â** (with), **tri** (three), and **chwe** (six):

c	>	**ch**	**tatws a chyw**	potatoes and chicken
p	>	**ph**	**bresych a phys**	cabbage and peas
t	>	**th**	**coffi a the**	coffee and tea
			tri chi	three dogs
			chwe phlentyn	six children
			tri thŷ	three houses
			chwe phunt	six pounds

GWERS UN DEG UN

LESSON ELEVEN

DEIALOG: SIOPA

Mae Janet a Mari wedi mynd i siopa. Maen nhw yn y dre, ac maen nhw wedi edrych ar lawer o siopau. Mae Janet wedi bod yn chwilio am anrhegion.

Mari: Mae'r siop ddillad yn llawn o bethau pert! Wyt ti'n moyn prynu dillad?

Janet: Ond pa faint? Dw i ddim yn gwybod pa faint i brynu? A dw i ddim eisiau prynu pethau trwm.

Mari: Wyt ti'n moyn prynu blowsys neu sgertiau i'r merched? Beth am sanau?

Janet: Mae digon o sgertiau 'da nhw. Ac mae digon o drowsusau 'da'r bechgyn. Beth yw pris y sanau?

Mari: Dwy bunt y pâr. Maen nhw'n ddrud. Beth am siacedi? Mae siacedi lliwgar yma.

Janet: Maen nhw'n cymryd gormod o le. Ond mae sgarffiau gwlân neis yma. Beth yw pris y sgarffiau?

Mari: Chwe phunt yr un. Maen nhw'n eitha rhad. Mae'r sgarffiau'n dod o ffatri wlân yn Sir Gaerfyrddin.

Janet: Iawn, rydw i'n mynd i brynu sgarff yr un i'r merched. Beth arall ydw i'n gallu prynu?

Mari: Wyt ti wedi meddwl am brynu llyfrau?

Janet: Mae llyfrau'n rhy drwm.

Mari: Beth am gasetiau a recordiau? Mae'r siop lyfrau rownd y gornel.

Janet: Syniad da.

Yn y siop lyfrau:

Siopwr: Ga i helpu?

Mari: Mae Janet yn chwilio am casetiau neu recordiau Cymraeg i fynd nôl i America.

Siopwr: Pa fath o gerddoriaeth ydych chi'n hoffi?

DIALOGUE: SHOPPING

Janet and Mari have gone shopping. They are in the town, and they have looked at many shops. Janet has been looking for presents.

Mari:	The clothes shop is full of pretty things! Do you want to buy clothes?
Janet:	But which size? I don't know which size to buy. And I don't want to buy heavy things.
Mari:	Do you want to buy blouses or skirts for the girls? What about socks?
Janet:	They have enough skirts. And the boys have enough trousers. What is the price of the socks?
Mari:	£2 a pair. They're expensive. What about jackets? There are colorful jackets here.
Janet:	They take too much space. But there are nice woollen scarves here. What is the price of the scarves?
Mari:	£6 each. They're quite cheap. The scarves come from a woollen factory in Carmarthenshire.
Janet:	Fine, I'm going to buy a scarf each for the girls. What else can I buy?
Mari:	Have you thought about books?
Janet:	Books are too heavy.
Mari:	What about cassettes and records? The book shop is around the corner.
Janet:	Good idea.

In the book shop:

Shopkeeper	May I help you?
Mari:	Janet is looking for Welsh cassettes or records to go back to America.
Shopkeeper:	What kind of music do you like?

Janet:	Wi'n hoffi caneuon gwerin. Oes casetiau caneuon gwerin 'da chi?
Siopwr:	Tapiau neu ddisgiau?
Janet:	Disgiau, os gwelwch yn dda. Beth yw pris y disgiau?
Siopwr:	Deuddeg punt yr un. Dafydd Iwan yw'r canwr mwya poblogaidd Ydych chi wedi clywed caneuon Meic Stevens?
Janet:	Ydw, rwy'n hoffi Meic Stevens—pedwar disg o ganeuon Dafydd Iwan, a thri disg o ganeuon Meic Stevens, os gwelwch yn dda.
Siopwr:	Dyna wyth deg pedwar punt.
Janet:	Ydych chi'n derbyn cerdyn American Express?

Janet: I like folk songs. Have you got folk songs?

Shopkeeper: Tapes or disks?

Janet: Disks, please. How much are the disks?

Shopkeeper: £12 each. Dafydd Iwan is the most popular singer.
                      Have you heard Meic Stevens' songs?

Janet: Yes, I like Meic Stevens—four disks of Dafydd Iwan
                      songs, and three disks of Meic Stevens' songs, please.

Shopkeeper: That's £84.

Janet: Do you accept an American Express card?

Ymadroddion a Geirfa / Phrases and Vocabulary

dillad (pl)	clothes
esgidiau (pl)	shoes
sanau (pl)	socks, stockings
trowsus (m)	trousers
sgert (f)	skirt
siwt (f)	suit
siaced (f)	jacket
blows (f)	blouse
bronglwm (m)	bra
crys (m)	shirt
tei (m)	tie
trons (m)	underpants
nicyrs (m)	knickers
sgarff (f)	scarf
bag (m)	bag
bag llaw	handbag
cês (m)	case
llestri (pl)	dishes
anrheg (f)	present
llyfr (m)	book
bwyd (m)	food
bisgedi (pl)	biscuits
siocled (m)	chocolate
llwy garu (f)	lovespoon
darlun (m)	picture
calendr (m)	calendar
syniad (m)	idea

GRAMADEG / GRAMMAR

Plurals

There are many ways of forming plurals of Welsh words. Here are some common endings added to words:

<table>
<tr><td align="center">-au</td><td align="center">-iau</td></tr>
<tr><td>gwelyau beds</td><td>darluniau pictures</td></tr>
<tr><td>calendrau calendars</td><td>lluniau pictures</td></tr>
<tr><td>llyfrau books</td><td>bagiau bags</td></tr>
<tr><td>crysau shirts</td><td>sgertiau skirts</td></tr>
<tr><td>llwyau spoons</td><td>esgidiau shoes</td></tr>
<tr><td>trowsusau trousers</td><td>plâtiau plates</td></tr>
<tr><td>papurau papers</td><td>ffilmiau films</td></tr>
<tr><td>wyau eggs</td><td>recordiau records</td></tr>
<tr><td>trên / trenau trains</td><td>casetiau cassettes</td></tr>
<tr><td>siopau shops</td><td></td></tr>
</table>

<table>
<tr><td align="center">-ion</td><td align="center">-i</td></tr>
<tr><td>dynion men</td><td>llestri dishes</td></tr>
<tr><td>anrhegion presents</td><td>siocledi chocolates</td></tr>
<tr><td></td><td>trefi towns</td></tr>
<tr><td></td><td>pentrefi villages</td></tr>
<tr><td></td><td>siacedi jackets</td></tr>
</table>

<table>
<tr><td align="center">-oedd</td><td align="center">-iaid</td></tr>
<tr><td>gwinoedd wines</td><td>anifail>anifeiliaid animals</td></tr>
<tr><td>strydoedd streets</td><td></td></tr>
<tr><td>dinasoedd cities</td><td></td></tr>
</table>

<table>
<tr><td align="center">-ys or -s</td></tr>
<tr><td>teis ties</td></tr>
<tr><td>blowsys blouses</td></tr>
<tr><td>cês / cesys cases</td></tr>
</table>

Others are more irregular or less common:

tŷ	>	tai	houses
car	>	ceir	cars
coeden	>	coed	trees
blodyn	>	blodau	flowers
fforc	>	ffyrc	forks
cyllell	>	cyllyll	knives
pysgodyn	>	pysgod	fish
bachgen	>	bechgyn	boys
gŵr	>	gwŷr	men
merch	>	marched	girls
ffermwr	>	ffermwyr	farmers

GEIRFA YCHWANEGOL / ADDITIONAL VOCABULARY

llawn o	full of
peth/au (m)	thing/s
trwm	heavy
lliwgar	colorful
gwlân (m)	wool
ffatri (f)	factory
drud	expensive
rhad	cheap
yr un	each
y pwys	per pound (in weight)
rhy	too (followed by soft mutation)
rownd	around
deuddeg	twelve (used with time and money)
caset/iau (m)	cassette/s
record/iau (f)	record/s
tâp>tapiau (m)	tape/s
canwr (m)	singer
cân>caneuon (f)	song/s
disg/iau (m)	disk/s

Ymarferion / Exercises

1. Use plural nouns in these sentences:

    Rwy'n prynu llyfr, caset a record.
    Mae hi wedi prynu tâp, sgert a sgarff i'r ferch.
    Maen nhw wedi prynu trowsus i'r bachgen.

2. Translate the following:

    £5 each.   £2 per pound.   £10 per pair.

3. Say that you have been shopping this morning. Say that you went to the clothes shop and the book shop. Say that you have bought a jacket, five books, and a tape.

Extra Grammar

'Too' with adjectives:

Rhy is followed by soft mutation, except for **ll** and **rh**:

Mae hi'n rhy boeth.	It is too hot.
Mae hi'n rhy ddrud.	It is too expensive.
Mae hi'n rhy rhad.	It is too cheap.

'Quite' with adjectives:

Eitha:

Mae e'n eitha da.	It's quite good.
Maen nhw'n eitha drud.	They're quite expensive.

'It':

As all nouns are feminine or masculine, 'it' must be translated either by **e** (he) or by **hi** (she), according to the gender of the noun:

Mae e (trowsus) yn rhad.   **Mae hi (sgert) yn ddrud.**

GWERS UN DEG DAU

LESSON TWELVE

Deialog: Yn Swyddfa'r Post

Mae Janet wedi mynd i Swyddfa'r Post. Mae hi eisiau anfon cardiau post a llythyrau i America.

Janet: Prynhawn da! Shwd ych chi?

Clerc: Prynhawn da! Yn dda iawn diolch. Ga i helpu?

Janet: Mae angen anfon llythyrau a chardiau i America arna i. Faint yw stamp i America?

Clerc: Llai na 10 gram, pedwar deg tri o geiniogau. Llai na dau ddeg gram, chwe deg tri o geiniogau.

Janet: Mae'n well i fi gael deg stamp pedwar deg tri o geiniogau, os gwelwch yn dda.

Clerc: Dyna bedair punt, tri deg ceiniog.

Janet: Ac mae angen postio pum llythyr arna i.

Clerc: Mae rhaid i fi bwyso'r llythyrau. Ydy'r llythyrau 'da chi?

Janet: Ydyn. Dyma nhw.

Clerc: Maen nhw i gyd o dan ddau ddeg gram. Dyna dair punt a phymtheg ceiniog. Cyfanswm o saith punt, pedwar deg pum ceiniog.

Janet: Dyma bapur deg punt.

Clerc: A dwy bunt pum deg pum ceiniog o newid.

Janet: Ydy hi'n bosibl i fi ffonio i America?

Clerc: Ydy, wrth gwrs, does dim problem. Mae'r ffôn yn y gornel. Ond mae'n well i chi brynu cerdyn ffôn.

Janet: Faint yw cerdyn ffôn?

Clerc: Dwy bunt, pum punt neu ddeg punt.

Janet: Un cerdyn am bum punt, os gwelwch yn dda.

Clerc: Dyma fe.

Janet: Mae hi'n hen bryd i fi ffonio America. Dw i ddim wedi ffonio'r plant ers wythnos. Mae bai arna i.

Clerc: Pob hwyl.

Janet: Pob hwyl a diolch.

DIALOGUE: AT THE POST OFFICE

Janet has gone to the Post Office. She wants to send postcards and letters to America.

Janet:　Good afternoon! How are you?

Clerk:　Good afternoon! Very well, thanks. May I help?

Janet:　I need to send letters and cards to America. How much is a stamp to America?

Clerk:　Less than 10g, 43 pence. Less than 20g, 63 pence.

Janet:　I'd better have ten 43p stamps, please.

Clerk:　That's £4.30p.

Janet:　And I need to post five letters.

Clerk:　I have to weigh the letters. Have you got the letters?

Janet:　Yes, here they are.

Clerk:　They are all under 20g. That's £3.15p. A total of £7.45p.

Janet:　Here's a £10 note.

Clerk:　And £2.55p change.

Janet:　Is it possible for me to telephone to America?

Clerk:　Yes, of course, there's no problem. The phone is in the corner. But you'd better buy a phone card.

Janet:　How much is a phone card?

Clerk:　£2, £5, or £10.

Janet:　One card at £5, please.

Clerk:　Here it is.

Janet:　It's about time I phoned America. I haven't phoned the children for a week. I'm at fault.

Clerk:　Good-bye.

Janet:　Good-bye and thanks.

YMADRODDION A GEIRFA / PHRASES AND VOCABULARY

stamp (m)	stamp
llythyr (m)	letter
amlen (f)	envelope
cerdyn (m)	card
cerdyn ffôn	phone card
postio	(to) post
pwyso	(to) weigh
post awyr	air mail
dosbarth cyntaf	first class
arian (m)	money
ail ddosbarth	second class
siec (f)	check
parsel (m)	parcel
ffôn (m)	telephone
ffonio	(to) telephone
talu	(to) pay
galwad ffôn (f)	telephone call
newid (m)	change
newid	(to) change

GRAMADEG / GRAMMAR

Some prepositions change their form according to the following pronoun:

i (to):

i fi	to me	**i ni**	to us
i ti	to you	**i chi**	to you
iddo fe	to him	**iddyn nhw**	to them
iddi hi	to her		

Phrases using **i** (to): the verb following **i** is soft mutated:

Mae'n	well	i fi	fynd	It's better for me to go.
	bryd	i ti	ffonio	It's time for you to phone.
	hen bryd	iddo fe	ddod	It's about time he came.
	rhaid	iddi hi	aros	She must stay.
	werth	i ni	aros	It's worth us waiting.
	bosibl	i chi	bostio	It's possible for you to post.
	hawdd	iddyn nhw	dalu	It's easy for them to pay.

ar (on):

arna i	on me	**arnon ni**	on us
arnat ti	on you	**arnoch chi**	on you
arno fe	on him	**arnyn nhw**	on them
arni hi	on her		

Phrases using **ar** (on):

Mae dyled arna i.	I am in debt.
Mae bai arna i.	I am at fault.
Mae annwyd arna i.	I have a cold.
Mae angen cot arna i.	I need a coat.
Mae hi ar ben arna i.	I'm finished.

o (of, from):

ohono i	of me	**ohonon ni**	of us
ohonot ti	of you	**ohonoch chi**	of you
ohono fe	of him	**ohonyn nhw**	of them
ohoni hi	of her		

Phrases using **o** (of):

With numbers higher than ten, **o** can be used, followed by plural nouns:

tri deg o blant   thirty children

GEIRFA YCHWANEGOL / ADDITIONAL VOCABULARY

llai na	less than
mwy na	more than
gwell na	better than
gwaeth na	worse than
gram (m)	gram
cyfanswm (m)	total
dim problem	no problem
ers	since, for
wythnos (f)	week
mis (m)	month
blwyddyn (f)	year
dydd (m)	day

YMARFERION / EXERCISES

1. Make up sentences using words from each of these columns:

Mae'n	rhaid well bryd hen bryd	i fi i chi iddo fe	brynu ffonio anfon	stampiau i America 'r plant llythyr cerdyn

2. a) Say you need five stamps at 43p.
    b) Say you want to telephone to America.
    c) Ask how much a phone card is.
    d) Ask where you can post letters.
    e) Say you are looking for the post office.

Extra Grammar

1. Note the changes in the following prepositions:

at (towards, to):

ata i	towards me	**aton ni**	towards us
atat ti	towards you	**atoch chi**	towards you
ato fe	towards him	**atyn nhw**	towards them
ati hi	towards her		

2. Note the following prepositions. All these are followed by soft mutation:

am	for, at	**dros**	over
gan	by, with	**trwy**	through
heb	without	**wrth**	by
dan	under	**hyd**	until

GWERS UN DEG TRI

LESSON THIRTEEN

DEIALOG: YN Y CAR

Mae Janet wedi llogi car am y penwythnos. Roedd hi a Mari
eisiau mynd i Fangor, ond maen nhw ar goll.

Janet:	Ydw i'n troi i'r chwith fan hyn?
Mari:	O daro, does dim syniad 'da fi ble ry'n ni.
Janet:	Ble oedden ni bore mae?
Mari:	Ro'n ni yn y Bala, wrth gwrs. Wedyn ro'n ni ar y ffordd i Ffestiniog. Wedyn ro'n ni ar y ffordd i Fangor.
Janet:	Ond roedd yr arwyddion yn glir. Dwyt ti ddim yn gallu darllen y map!
Mari:	Ond doedd yr arwyddion ddim yn glir. Do't ti ddim yn gwybod ble i fynd chwaith.
Janet:	O wel, roedd y daith yn braf.
Mari:	Ac ro'n ni wedi cael bwyd da yn y Bala.
Janet:	O't ti wedi cael oen?
Mari:	O'n. Roedd e'n flasus iawn.
Janet:	Wel, mae'n well i ni fynd i'r garej i gael petrol ac i ofyn y ffordd.

Yn y garej.

Janet:	Chwe galwyn o petrol, os gwelwch yn dda.
Dyn y garej:	Croeso. Oes angen olew arnoch chi?
Janet:	Na, mae digon o olew yn y car. Ond wi am roi awyr yn y teiars.
Dyn y gareg:	Dim problem. Mae'r peiriant ar y dde. Unrhyw beth arall?
Janet:	Oes. Ry'n ni ar goll. Beth yw'r ffordd orau i fynd i Fangor?
Dyn y garej:	Dy'ch chi ddim yn bell. Trowch i'ch chwith i'r ffordd fawr, wedyn i'r dde.

DIALOGUE: IN THE CAR

Janet has hired a car for the weekend. She and Mari wanted to go to Bangor, but they are lost.

Janet:	Do I turn left here?
Mari:	Oh dear, I've got no idea where we are.
Janet:	Where were we this morning?
Mari:	We were in Bala. Then we were on the way to Ffestiniog. Then we were on the way to Bangor.
Janet:	But the signs were clear! You can't read the map.
Mari:	But the signs were not clear. You didn't know where to go either.
Janet:	Oh well, the journey was fine.
Mari:	And we had good food in Bala.
Janet:	Did you have lamb?
Mari:	Yes. It was very tasty.
Janet:	Well, we'd better go to the garage to have petrol and to ask the way.

In the garage.

Janet:	Six gallons of petrol, please.
Garage man:	Welcome. Do you need oil?
Janet:	No, there's enough oil in the car. But I want to put air in the tires.
Garage man:	No problem. The machine is on the right. Anything else?
Janet:	Yes. We're lost. What is the best way to go to Bangor?
Garage man:	You're not far. Turn to the left to the main road, then to the right.

Janet:	Pa mor bell yw Bangor?
Dyn y garej:	Ugain milltir. Ydych chi eisiau prynu map?
Janet:	Na, mae map 'da ni, diolch.
Mari:	Diolch byth, dy'n ni ddim wedi torri lawr.

Janet: How far is Bangor?
Garage man: Twenty miles. Do you want to buy a map?
Janet: No, we have a map, thanks.
Mari: Thank goodness, we haven't broken down.

YMADRODDION A GEIRFA / PHRASES AND VOCABULARY

petrol (m)	petrol, gasoline
galwyn (m)	gallon
olew (m)	oil
teiar (m)	tire
awyr (f)	air
pwysedd (m)	pressure
sedd flaen (f)	front seat
sedd gefn (f)	back seat
llogi	(to) hire
torri lawr	(to) break down
gwasnanaethau	services
heol (f)	road
traffordd (f)	motorway
taith (f)	journey
milltir (f)	mile
modurdy (m)	garage
garej (f)	garage
gorsaf betrol (f)	petrol station
arwydd (f/m)	sign
dim aros	no waiting
ffordd fawr (f)	main road
map (m)	map
golau (m)	light
goleuadau (pl)	lights
gyrrwr (m)	driver
tacsi (m)	taxi
gyrru	(to) drive

GRAMADEG / GRAMMAR

Past tense: imperfect

Was, were:

To say that something was happening, or that things were going on, use **roedd** instead of **mae**:

Mae'r bws yn dod.	The bus is coming.
Roedd y bws yn dod.	The bus was coming.

Here is a full list:

Roeddwn	**i'n**	**mynd**	I was going.
Roeddet	**ti'n**	**gyrru**	You were driving.
Roedd	**e'n**	**cerdded**	He was walking.
Roedd	**hi'n**	**aros**	She was waiting.
Roedd	**Sian yn**	**mynd**	Sian was going.
Roedd	**y plant yn**	**chwarae**	The children were playing.
Roedden	**ni'n**	**dod**	We were coming.
Roeddech	**chi'n**	**cysgu**	You were sleeping.

Alternative forms of the above, especially when talking:

Roeddwn i	→	**Ro'n i**
Roeddet ti	→	**Ro't ti**
Roedd e	→	**Ro'dd e**
Roedd hi	→	**Ro'dd hi**
Roedden ni	→	**Ro'n ni**
Roeddech chi	→	**Ro'ch chi**
Roedden nhw	→	**Ro'n nhw**

To ask questions, simply drop the first **r**:

O'ch chi'n gyrru?	Were you driving?	**O'n.**	Yes.	**Na.**	No.
O'dd hi'n aros?	Was she waiting?	**O'dd.**	Yes.	**Na.**	No.
Oedd e'n mynd?	Was he going?	**Oedd.**	Yes.	**Na .**	No.

GEIRFA YCHWANEGOL / ADDITIONAL VOCABULARY

penwythnos (m)	weekend
gogledd	north
de	south
ar goll	lost
fan hyn	here
wedyn	then
arwyddion (pl)	signs
clir	clear
chwaith	either
blasus	tasty
peiriant (m)	machine, engine
gorau	best
pa mor bell?	how far?
diolch byth	thank goodness

YMARFERION / EXERCISES

1. Make up sentences using words from the following columns:

Ro'n	i'n	gyrru	yn y car	i Fangor
		dal	y bws	i Fethesda
		mynd	yn y trên	i Aberystwyth
		cerdded	ar y ffordd	i'r Bala
		rhedeg	ar yr heol	i Gaernarfon

2. Say where you went on vacation last year:

Ro'n i	yn	yr Almaen	Germany
		Ewrop	Europe
		yr Eidal	Italy
		yr Unol Daleithiau	the United States
		gartre	at home

Extra Grammar

1. How to say you were not (imperfect negative):

   Put **d** instead of **r**, and insert **ddim** after the subject:

Do'n i ddim yn gyrru.	I wasn't driving.
Do'dd e ddim yno.	He wasn't there.
Do'n ni ddim yn yfed.	We weren't drinking.
Do'n ni ddim ar goll.	We weren't lost.
Doedd Huw ddim yn cysgu.	Hugh wasn't sleeping.

2. How to say you 'had' done something (pluperfect):

   Simply put **wedi** instead of **yn**:

Ro'n i wedi gyrru.	I had driven.
Do'n ni ddim wedi yfed.	We had not drunk.
Doedd Huw ddim wedi cysgu.	Huw had not slept.
Ro'n i wedi cael cinio.	I had had dinner.
O'ch chi wedi gweld y ffilm?	Had you seen the film? / Did you see the film?

GWERS UN DEG PEDWAR

LESSON FOURTEEN

Deialog: Yn y Wlad

Ar ôl aros ym Mangor, roedd Janet a Mari wedi mynd i Sir Fôn. Roedden nhw eisiau gwersylla.

Mari:	Edrycha! Mae'r wlad yn hyfryd. Wyt ti'n hoffi ein gwlad ni?
Janet:	Ydw, mae'r mynyddoedd a'r coed yn ogoneddus.
Mari:	Wyt ti wedi cofio dy babell di?
Janet:	Ydw, mae'r babell yn fy nghar i. Pabell fy mrawd i yw hi. Edrycha! Mae arwydd gwersyll fan'na.
Mari:	Oes. Mae'r gwersyll yn y fferm. Gyrra i mewn.
Ffermwr:	Prynhawn da! Ydych chi am wersylla fan hyn?
Mari:	Ydyn, os gwelwch yn dda.
Ffermwr:	Wel, bydd digon o gwmni i chi fan hyn; edrychwch ar fy anifeiliaid i, fy muchod i, fy moch i, fy nefaid i ... maen nhw i gyd yn aros amdanoch chi.
Mari:	Faint yw cost pabell a dau oedolyn am ddwy noson?
Ffermwr:	Pum punt am babell, dwy bunt y person: dyna naw punt y noson.
Janet:	Oes tai bach a chawod yn y gwersyll?
Ffermwr:	Oes, mae ein cyfleusterau ni wrth y ffermdy.

Yn y nos:

Mari:	Wyt ti wedi deffro? Wyt ti ar ddihun?
Janet:	Cysga, er mwyn popeth!
Mari:	Dwi i ddim yn gallu cysgu. Mae 'mhen i'n dost. Mae annwyd arna i.
Janet:	Beth yw'r sŵn yna?
Mari:	O na, yr anifeiliaid! Mae'r ffermwr yn cysgu'n hapus, ond mae ei fuchod e, ei geffylau fe, ei gathod e, ei foch e i gyd yn cadw sŵn!
Janet:	Rwy'n mynd i gwyno yn y bore.
Mari:	Rwy'n codi nawr. Dere, dere i gwyno nawr.

DIALOGUE: IN THE COUNTRY

After staying in Bangor, Janet and Mari went to Anglesey. They
wanted to camp.

Mari: Look! The country is lovely. Do you like our country?

Janet: Yes, the mountains and the trees are wonderful.

Mari: Have you remembered your tent?

Janet: Yes, the tent is in my car. It's my brother's tent. Look!
          There is a camping sign over there.

Mari: Yes. The camp is in the farm. Drive in.

Farmer: Good afternoon! Do you want to camp here?

Mari: Yes, please.

Farmer: Well, there'll be enough company for you here; look at
          my animals, my cows, my pigs, my sheep ... they are all
          waiting for you.

Mari: How much is the cost of a tent and two adults for two nights?

Farmer: Five pounds for a tent, £2 per person: that is £9 per night.

Janet: Are there toilets and a shower in the camp?

Farmer: Yes, our facilities are by the farmhouse.

In the night:

Mari: Have you woken up? Are you awake?

Janet: Go to sleep, for goodness' sake.

Mari: I can't sleep. My head is ill. I have a cold.

Janet: What is that noise?

Mari: Oh, no, the animals! The farmer is sleeping happily, but his
          cows, his horses, his cats, his pigs are all making noise!

Janet: I'm going to complain in the morning.

Mari: I'm getting up now. Come, come to complain now.

YMADRODDION A GEIRFA / PHRASES AND VOCABULARY

cae (m) / caeau	field /s
afon (f) / afonydd	river /s
nant (m) / nentydd	brook /s
mynydd (m) / mynyddoedd	mountain /s
clawdd (m) / cloddiau	hedge /s
blodyn (m) / blodau	flower /s
anifail (m) / anifeiliaid	animal /s
ceffyl (m) / ceffylau	horse /s
ci (m) / cŵn	dog /s
cath (f) / cathod	cat /s
cyw (m) / cywion	chicken /s
coeden (f) / coed	tree /s
llyn (m) / llynnoedd	lake /s
bryn (m) / bryniau	hill /s
gwersyll (m) / gwersylloedd	camp /s
aderyn (m) / adar	bird /s
dafad (f) / defaid	sheep
buwch (f) / buchod	cow /s
iâr (f) / ieir	hen /s
mochyn (m) / moch	pig /s
pabell (f) / pebyll	tent /s
fferm (f) / ffermydd	farm /s

GRAMADEG / GRAMMAR

Commands

When talking to more than one person, or a person you do not know well, add -**wch** to the stem of the verb. The stem is usually found by dropping off the last vowel; some verbs are more irregular. When talking to a person you know well, add **a** to the stem of the verb:

Verb		Plural/Formal Command	Singular Command	Meaning
cysgu	→	cysgwch	cysga	go to sleep!
codi	→	codwch	coda	get up!
edrych	→	edrychwch	edrycha	look!
eistedd	→	eisteddwch	eistedda	sit down!
dod	→	dewch	dere	come!
mynd	→	ewch	cer	go!
gwneud	→	gwnewch	gwna	do or make!

Possessive pronouns

My, your, his, her, our, their:

These have two elements in Welsh: the first is put before the noun, and the second after it. It is possible to use the first on its own. Some of them cause mutations.

For example:
ci dog

fy ... i	my	**fy nghi i**	my dog	(+ nasal mutation)
dy ... di	your	**dy gi di**	your dog	(+ soft mutation)
ei ... e	his	**ei gi e**	his dog	(+ soft mutation)
ei ... hi	her	**ei chi hi**	her dog	(+ aspirate mutation)
ein ... ni	our	**ein ci ni**	our dog	(no mutation)
eich ... chi	your	**eich ci chi**	your dog	(no mutation)
eu ... nhw	their	**eu ci nhw**	their dog	(no mutation)

Geirfa Ychwanegol / Additional Vocabulary

ym Mangor	in Bangor
Sir Fôn	Anglesey
gwersylla	(to) camp
gogoneddus	wonderful
fan'na	over there
cwmni (m)	company
brawd (m)	brother
chwaer (f)	sister
tad (m)	father
mam (f)	mother
aros am	(to) wait for
oedolyn (m)	adult
tai bach (pl)	toilets
deffro	(to) wake up
ar ddihun	awake
yn dost	ill
hapus	happy
er mwyn popeth	for goodness' sake
i gyd	all (used after the noun)
cadw sŵn	(to) make noise
cwyno	complain

Ymarferion / Exercises

1. Put **fy ... i** around the following words (see extra grammar on page 155 first):

    tad
    pentref
    tref
    dinas
    gwlad
    gwely
    pabell
    car
    basged

2. Make up sentences using words from the following columns (note that the **i** has been omitted; the meaning is the same):

Mae	fy	nghath	yn	dost
		nghi		hapus
Roedd		ngheffyl		cysgu
		muwch		cadw swn

Extra Grammar

1. Nasal mutation. These are the changes:

c	>	ngh	car	>	fy nghar i	my car
p	>	mh	pentref	>	fy mhentref i	my village
t	>	nh	tŷ	>	fy nhŷ	my house
g	>	ng	gwlad	>	fy ngwlad i	my country
b	>	m	basged	>	fy masged i	my basket
d	>	n	dant	>	fy nant i	my tooth

2. The nasal mutation occurs after the following:

a) after **fy** (my), as above, and
b) after **yn** (in; note the various forms of **yn**):

Caerdydd	>	yng Nghaerdydd	in Cardiff
Paris	>	ym Mharis	in Paris
Talybont	>	yn Nhalybont	in Talybont
Gwent	>	yng Ngwent	in Gwent
Bangor	>	ym Mangor	in Bangor
Dinbych	>	yn Ninbych	in Denbigh
Cymru	>	yng Nghymru	in Wales

GWERS UN DEG PUMP

LESSON FIFTEEN

DEIALOG: GYDA'R MEDDYG

Mae Janet yn gwybod ei bod hi'n dost.

Mari: Mae'n well i ti weld y meddyg.
Janet: Ond dw i ddim eisiau ei weld e.
Mari: Mae'n rhaid i ti. Rwy'n credu bod meddyg yn y pentref.

Maen nhw'n mynd i'r feddygfa.

Meddyg: Dewch i mewn. Beth sy'n bod arnoch chi?
Janet: Rwy'n credu bod gwres arna i. Mae peswch arna i, ac mae annwyd arna i, ac mae pen tost arna i.
Meddyg: Ydych chi'n credu bod ffliw arnoch chi?
Janet: Rwy'n credu ei fod e arna i, ond dw i ddim yn siŵr.
Meddyg: Mae rhaid i fi gymryd eich gwres chi. Oes, mae gwres arnoch chi. Rwy'n siŵr bod ffliw arnoch chi.
Janet: Beth ydw i'n gallu gwneud nawr?
Meddyg: Rydw i'n mynd i roi papur meddyg i chi. Cymerwch y moddion tair gwaith y dydd. Byddwch chi'n well ar ôl tri dydd.
Janet: Sut ydw i'n gallu'ch talu chi?
Meddyg: Oes yswiriant 'da chi?
Janet: Oes, rwy'n siŵr bod yswiriant 'da fi.
Meddyg: Wel, dyma ffurflen. Llanwch y ffurflen, os gwelwch yn dda.
Janet: Enw cyntaf, Janet; Cyfenw Hughes; Cyfeiriad, 1 State Gardens; Rhif yswiriant, un, dau, saith, pump, pedwar. Dyna ni.
Meddyg: Diolch yn fawr. Ewch â'r ffurflen yn ôl i America, a bydd yr yswiriant yn talu.
Janet: Diolch yn fawr. Wi'n mynd i aros mewn gwesty heno. Rwy'n credu 'mod i wedi cael hen ddigon o wersylla.

DIALOGUE: AT THE DOCTOR'S

Janet knows that she is ill.

Mari: You'd better see the doctor.

Janet: But I don't want to see him.

Mari: You must. I think that there is a doctor in the village.

They go to the doctor's office.

Doctor: Come in. What's the matter with you?

Janet: I think that I have a temperature. I have a cough, and I have a cold, and I have a headache.

Doctor: Do you think that you have the flu?

Janet: I think I have it, but I'm not sure.

Doctor: I must take your temperature. Yes, you have a temperature. I'm sure that you have the flu.

Janet: What can I do now?

Doctor: I'm going to give you a prescription. Take the medicine three times a day. You'll be better after three days.

Janet: How can I pay you?

Doctor: Have you got insurance?

Janet: Yes, I'm sure that I have insurance.

Doctor: Well, here's a form. Fill out the form, please.

Janet: First name, Janet; surname, Hughes; address, 1 State Gardens; insurance number, one, two, seven, five, four. There we are.

Doctor: Thank you very much. Take the form back to America, and the insurance will pay.

Janet: Thank you very much. I'm going to stay in a hotel tonight. I think that I've had enough of camping.

YMADRODDION A GEIRFA / PHRASES AND VOCABULARY

meddyg (m)	doctor
meddygfa (f)	doctor's office
pen tost (m)	headache
llygad (m) / llygaid	eye /s
braich (f) / breichiau	arm /s
coes (f) / coesau	leg /s
clust (f) / clustiau	ear /s
llaw (f) / dwylo	hand /s
bys (m) / bysedd	finger /s
enw (m) / enwau	name /s
tabled (m) / tabledi	pill, tablet /s
papur meddyg (m)	prescription
ceg (f)	mouth
tafod (m)	tongue
brest (f)	chest
enw cyntaf	first name
cyfenw (m)	surname
cyfeiriad (m)	address
yswiriant (m)	insurance
moddion (pl)	medicine
gwallt (pl)	hair
trwyn (m)	nose
troed (f) / traed	foot / feet
llwnc (m)	throat

GRAMADEG / GRAMMAR

Pronoun object of the verb

The forms of the possessive pronoun are used as the object of the verb:

talu   (to) pay:

Mae e wedi	fy nhalu i dy dalu di ei dalu e ei thalu hi ein talu ni eich talu chi eu talu nhw	He has	paid me paid you paid him paid her paid us paid you paid them

Pronouns in noun clauses

The noun clause introduced by 'that' in English, (for example, I know *that* he is coming) is introduced by **bod** in Welsh, followed by **yn** or **wedi** with verbs:

I know *that the bus is coming.* **Rwy'n gwybod *bod y bws yn dod.***
I know *that the bus has come.* **Rwy'n gwybod *bod y bws wedi dod.***

When used with pronouns, the same forms as the possessive pronouns are used, and are put around the word **bod**:

fy mod i	that I am	**ein bod ni**	that we are
dy fod ti	that you are	**eich bod chi**	that you are
ei fod e	that he is	**eu bod nhw**	that they are
ei bod hi	that she is		

For example:
I know that he is coming. **Rwy'n gwybod ei fod e'n dod.**
I know that he has come. **Rwy'n gwybod ei fod e wedi dod.**

GEIRFA YCHWANEGOL / ADDITIONAL VOCABULARY

ei bod hi'n	that she is
gwres (m)	temperature, fever
ffliw (m)	flu
cymryd	(to) take
tair gwaith	three times
y dydd	a day
byddwch	you'll be
ffurflen (f)	form
llanwch	fill (in)
rhif (m)	number
ewch â	take
hen ddigon	enough by far

YMARFERION / EXERCISES

1. Put **fy ... i** (my) around these words:

   For example:
   car – fy nghar i

   tad
   gwlad
   cinio
   pen
   coes

   Put **ei ... e** (his) around these words:

   For example:
   pen – ei ben e

   tŷ
   gardd
   papur
   mam
   tref

2. Say that you know something:

For example:
I know *that the bus is coming.*   **Wi'n gwybod** *bod y bws yn dod.*

... that I have a cold   ... that I am ill
... that I am coming   ... that I am staying in a hotel
... that he can pay   ... that she has insurance

3. Translate these:

I am paying her.
The doctor sees her.
The man has dinner and eats it.
She asks for a glass of wine and drinks it all.

Extra Grammar

To form the negative noun clause, insert **ddim**:

Examples:
Wi'n gwybod bod y   **Wi'n gwybod bod y car**
  car yn dod.   *ddim* **yn dod.**
I know that the car   I know that the car
  is coming.   isn't coming.

Wi'n credu ei bod   **Wi'n credu ei bod**
  hi'n talu.   **hi** *ddim* **yn talu.**

fy mod i ddim   that I'm not
dy fod ti ddim   that you're not
ei fod e ddim   that he's not
ei bod hi ddim   that she's not
bod Huw ddim   that Hugh isn't
bod y plant ddim   that the children aren't
ein bod ni ddim   that we are not
eich bod chi ddim   that you're not
eu bod nhw ddim   that they're not

GWERS UN DEG CHWECH

LESSON SIXTEEN

DEIALOG: MYND I'R GÊM

Aeth Janet i weld gêm bêl-droed, ond dyw hi ddim yn deall
y gêm.

Janet: Ceson ni lwc: mae sedd dda 'da ni.
Mari: Oes, fe brynes i'r tocynnau ddoe.
Janet: Faint costion nhw?
Mari: Fe gostion nhw wyth punt yr un.
Janet: Weloch chi'r chwaraewr yna.
Mari: Do.
Janet: Beth wnaeth e?
Mari: Sgoriodd e gôl, wrth gwrs.
Janet: Ydy Abertawe'n chwarae'n dda?
Mari: Ydyn. Fe enillon nhw'r wythnos ddiwethaf, ond collon
        nhw nos Fercher.
Janet: Faint sgorion nhw yn yr hanner cyntaf?
Mari: Fe sgorion nhw dri gôl.
Janet: A faint sgoriodd Caerdydd?
Mari: Fe sgorion nhw un gôl.
Janet: Edrych! Fe sgoriodd un o chwaraewyr Caerydd!
Mari: Naddo! Fe gafodd Abertawe gic rydd.
Janet: O diar, cic rydd, cic gosb, dw i ddim yn deall y gêm.
Mari: Paid â phoeni! Dim ond gêm yw hi!
Janet: Fe weles i Atlanta Braves yn chwarae. Rwy'n deall
        pêl-fas.
Mari: Weles i mo nhw, a dw i ddim yn deall pêl-fas.
Janet: Wel, mae pêl-fas yn gyffrous iawn. Mae un tîm yn batio,
        ac yn ceisio rhedeg o gwmpas y cylch, ac mae'r tîm arall
        yn taflu'r bêl, ac wedyn yn ceisio dal y bêl...
Mari: Edrych! Fe sgoriodd Abertawe eto!
Janet: O diar, fe golles i'r gôl yna.

DIALOGUE: GOING TO THE GAME

Janet went to see a football game, but she doesn't understand
the game.

Janet: We had some luck: we've got a good seat.
Mari: Yes, I bought the tickets yesterday.
Janet: How much did they cost?
Mari: They cost £8 each.
Janet: Did you see that player?
Mari: Yes.
Janet: What did he do?
Mari: He scored a goal, of course.
Janet: Is Swansea playing well?
Mari: Yes. They won last week, but they lost on Wednesday night.

Janet: How much did they score in the first half?
Mari: They scored three goals.
Janet: And how much did Cardiff score?
Mari: They scored one goal.
Janet: Look! One of Cardiff's players scored!
Mari: No! Swansea had a free kick.
Janet: Oh dear, free kick, penalty, I don't understand the game.
Mari: Don't worry! It's only a game!
Janet: I saw the Atlanta Braves playing. I understand baseball.

Mari: I didn't see them, and I don't understand baseball.
Janet: Well, baseball is very exciting. One team bats, and tries to
         run around the circle, and the other team throws the ball, and
         then tries to catch the ball...
Mari: Look! Swansea scored again!
Janet: Oh dear, I missed that goal.

YMADRODDION A GEIRFA / PHRASES AND VOCABULARY

gêm (f)	game
sgôr (m/f)	score
rygbi (m)	rugby
hoci (m)	hockey
pêl-droed (f)	football
gôl (m/f)	goal
ennill	(to) win
colli	(to) lose
tennis (m)	tennis
nofio	(to) swim
golff (m)	golf
cae (m)	field
hanner (m)	half
hanner cyntaf	first half
ail hanner	second half
chwaraewr (m)	player
chwaraewyr	players
cyfartal	drawn

GRAMADEG / GRAMMAR

Past tense, short form

These endings are added to the verb's stem:

Endings	Verb stem "saw" & ending *gweld* 'I saw', etc.	Verb stem "bought" & ending *prynu* 'I bought', etc.
...es i	gweles i	prynes i
...est ti	gwelest ti	prynest ti
...odd e	gwelodd e	prynodd e
...odd hi	gwelodd hi	prynodd hi
...odd Huw	gwelodd Huw	prynodd Huw
...odd y plant	gwelodd y plant	prynoddy plant
...on ni	gwelon ni	prynon ni
...och chi	gweloch chi	prynoch chi
...on nhw	gwelon nhw	prynon nhw

Endings	Verb stem "got up" & ending *codi* 'I got up', etc.	Verb stem "read" & ending *darllen* 'I read', etc.
...es i	codes i	darllenes i
...est ti	codest ti	darllenest ti
...odd e	cododd e	darllenodd e
...odd hi	cododd hi	darllenodd hi
...odd Huw	cododd Huw	darllenodd Huw
...odd y plant	cododd y plant	darllenodd y plant
...on ni	codon ni	darllenon ni
...och chi	codoch chi	darllenoch chi
...on nhw	codon nhw	darllenon nhw

Mynd (to go), **dod** (to come), **cael** (to have), and **gwneud** (to do) are irregular:

    mynd (to go):
      es i
      est ti
      aeth e
      aeth hi
      aeth Huw
      aeth y plant
      aethon ni
      aethoch chi
      aethon nhw

    dod (to come):
      des i
      dest ti
      daeth e
      daeth hi
      daeth Huw
      daeth y plant
      daeth ni
      daeth chi
      daeth nhw

    gwneud (to do):
      gwnes i
      gwnest ti
      gwnaeth e
      gwnaeth hi
      gwnaeth Huw
      gwnaeth y plant
      gwnaeth ni
      gwnaeth chi
      gwnaeth nhw

cael (to have):
 ces i
 cest ti
 cafodd e
 cafodd hi
 cafodd Huw
 cafodd y plant
 ceson ni
 cesoch chi
 ceson nhw

The object of the short form of the verb is soft mutated:

Darllenes i lyfr	I read a book.
(Darllenes i'r llyfr.)	(I read the book.)
Prynes i docyn.	I bought a ticket.
(Prynes i'r tocyn.)	(I bought the ticket.)

Questions

Simply mutate the first letter of the verb, if it can be mutated:

Prynoch chi docyn.	You bought a ticket.		
Brynoch chi docyn?	Did you buy a ticket?	**Do.**	Yes.
Gweloch chi'r gêm.	You saw the game.		
Weloch chi'r gêm?	Did you see the game?	**Na** *or* **Naddo.**	No.

GEIRFA YCHWANEGOL / ADDITIONAL VOCABULARY

lwc (f)	luck
sedd (f)	seat
fe	[no meaning; it confirms the verb, and causes soft mutation]
diwethaf	last
nos Fercher	Wednesday night
batio	(to) bat
sgorio	(to) score
cic rydd (f)	free kick

cic gosb (f)	free kick, penalty
dim ond (f)	only
pêl-fas	baseball
cyffrous	exciting
yna	that (**yma** – this)
eto	again
colli	miss, lose
ceisio	(to) try (to)

Ymarferion / Exercises

1. Make as many sentences as possible using words from these
    columns:

Gweles i	Huw Abertawe Gaerdydd	yn chwarae yn ennill yn colli	yn y gêm pêl-droed y gêm 'r gêm

2. Say you did the following things:

saw the doctor	scored a goal	bought a ticket
went to the game	won the game	lost the ticket

Extra Grammar

1. Negative of past tense, short form:

    a) Insert **ddim** after the verb. Aspirate the mutation of the first
        letter of the verb where possible; otherwise, soft mutation
        occurs:

Prynes i docyn.	> **Phrynes i ddim tocyn.**	I didn't buy a ticket.
Gweles i gêm.	> **Weles i ddim gêm.**	I didn't see a game.

b) Before names of people and the definite article (**y**, **'r**), insert **mo** after the verb:

Prynes i'r tocyn. > **Phrynes i mo'r tocyn.**	I didn't buy the ticket.
Gweles i'r game. > **Weles i mo'r gêm.**	I didn't see the game.
Gweles i Huw. > **Weles i mo Huw.**	I didn't see Huw.

2. Showing possession:

When two nouns follow each other, the first is usually 'owned' by the second:

cap y bachgen	the boy's cap
tîm Abertawe	Swansea's team
llyfr Sian	Sian's book

There is no need to translate the ''s' seen in English.

GWERS UN DEG SAITH

LESSON SEVENTEEN

DEIALOG: YN SWYDDFA'R HEDDLU

Mae Janet wedi dal trên o Fangor i Gaerdydd. Ond collodd hi ei bag llaw ar y trên. Mae hi'n awr yn swyddfa'r heddlu.

Janet: O diar, rwy wedi colli fy arian.

Plismon: Pryd colloch chi e?

Janet: Colles i fe ar y trên.

Plismon: Sut colloch chi fe?

Janet: Mae e wedi cael ei ddwyn.

Plismon: Wedi cael ei ddwyn?

Janet: Ydy. Roedd yr arian wedi cael ei roi yn fy mag llaw.

Plismon: Ydy'r bag llaw wedi cael ei ddwyn hefyd?

Janet: Ydy, mae f'arian i wedi cael ei ddwyn, fy mag i wedi cael ei ddwyn.

Plismon: Oes unrhyw beth arall wedi cael ei ddwyn?

Janet: Oes. Roedd llawer o bethau yn y bag.

Plismon: Beth?

Janet: Roedd persawr 'da fi, allweddi—maen nhw i gyd wedi cael eu dwyn.

Plismon: Pryd oedd popeth wedi cael ei ddwyn?

Janet: Ro'n i'n cysgu yn y trên. Roedd dau fachgen bach wedi cael eu gweld yn y trên. Roedd un bachgen wedi cael ei weld yn y tŷ bach, ac roedd un bachgen wedi cael ei weld yn y coridor.

Plismon: Aha! Mae'r bag wedi cael ei ffeindio. Mae e wedi cael ei roi i ni gan y ddau fachgen. Ro'n nhw wedi ei weld e ar y llawr yn y trên.

DIALOGUE: AT THE POLICE STATION

Janet has caught a train from Bangor to Cardiff. But she lost her handbag on the train. She is now at the police station.

Janet:	Oh dear, I've lost my money.
Policeman:	When did you lose it?
Janet:	I lost it on the train.
Policeman:	How did you lose it?
Janet:	It's been stolen.
Policeman:	Been stolen?
Janet:	Yes. The money had been put in my handbag.
Policeman:	Has the handbag been stolen too?
Janet:	Yes, my money has been stolen, my bag has been stolen.
Policeman:	Has anything else been stolen?
Janet:	Yes. There were many things in the bag.
Policeman:	What?
Janet:	I had perfume, keys—they have all been stolen.
Policeman:	When had everything been stolen?
Janet:	I was sleeping in the train. Two boys had been seen in the train. One boy had been seen in the toilet, and one boy had been seen in the corridor.
Policeman:	Aha! The bag has been found. The bag has been given to us by two boys. They had seen it on the floor in the train.

Mae Janet yn ysgrifennu llythyr adre:

Annwyl Sion a Sian,

Rwy wedi cael amser da yng Nghymru. Mae'r tywydd wedi bod yn dda. Mae'r wlad yn hyfryd. Mae'r mynyddoedd yn brydferth, ac mae'r trefi'n ddiddorol.

Ond heddiw yn y trên roedd fy mag i wedi cael ei ddwyn, ond diolch byth, mae'r bag wedi cael ei ffeindio.

Rwy'n dod nôl i America mewn wythnos.

Cofion gorau,
Mam

Janet is writing a letter home:

Dear Sion and Sian,

I have had a good time in Wales. The weather has been good.
The country is nice. The mountains are beautiful, and the towns are
interesting.

But today in the train my bag had been stolen, but thank goodness, it has been found.

I'm coming back to America in a week.

Fond regards,
Mom

Ymadroddion a Geirfa / Phrases and Vocabulary

plismon (m)	policeman
swyddfa (f)	office
dal	(to) catch
colli	(to) lose
lleidr (m)	thief
dwyn	(to) steal
cael ei ddal	to be caught (he)
cael ei dal	to be caught (she)
bag llaw (m)	handbag

Gramadeg / Grammar

Use **cael** for 'be' to express 'to be caught'. **Cael** is followed by forms of the possessive pronoun. This is followed by the verb, mutated:

dal to catch

Rwy'n	cael	fy	nal	I am (being) caught
Rwyt ti'n		dy	ddal	You're (being) caught
Mae e'n		ei	ddal	He's (being) caught
Mae hi'n		ei	dal	She's (being) caught
Mae Sian yn		ei	dal	Sian is (being) caught
Mae'r plant yn	cael	eu	dal	The children are caught
Ry'n ni'n		ein	dal	We're (being) caught
Ry'ch chi'n		eich	dal	You're (being) caught
Maen nhw'n		(eu)	dal	They're (being) caught

In the past tense, 'n is replaced by **wedi**:

gweld to see

Rwy	wedi	cael	fy	ngweld	I have been seen
Rwyt ti			dy	weld	You've been seen
Mae e			ei	weld	He's been seen
Mae hi			ei	gweld	She's been seen
Mae Huw			ei	weld	Huw has been seen
Mae'r plant			eu	gweld	The children have been seen
Ry'n ni			ein	gweld	We've been seen
Ry' ch chi			eich	gweld	You've been seen
Maen nhw			eu	gweld	They've been seen

Questions and answers follow the usual pattern:

Ydych chi wedi cael eich dal? Have you been caught?
 Ydw.   Yes.
 Na.   No.

Negative sentences also follow the usual pattern:

Dw i ddim wedi cael fy nal. I haven't been caught.

GEIRFA YCHWANEGOL / ADDITIONAL VOCABULARY

persawr (m)	perfume
allweddi (pl)	keys
coridor (m)	corridor
nodyn (m)	note
gan	by
annwyl (a)	dear
prydferth	beautiful
ffeindio	(to) find
cofion gorau	fond regards

Other ways of finishing a letter:

Pob hwyl	All the best
Cariad mawr	Lots of love
Yn gywir	Yours sincerely
Dymuniadau gorau	Best wishes

YMARFERION / EXERCISES

1. Make sentences using words from the following columns:

Mae'r	bwyd	wedi	cael	ei fwyta
	gwin	yn		ei yfed
	tocyn			ei brynu
	gêm			ei chwarae
	bag			ei ddwyn
				ei ffeindio

2. Say the following in Welsh:

a) The bread has been eaten.
b) The book has been read.
c) The film has been seen.
d) The bag has been lost.

Extra Grammar

1. To say that something had been done, replace **mae** with **roedd**, **'rwy** with **ro'n**, etc.:

Ro'n i wedi cael fy ngweld.	I had been seen.
Ro't ti wedi cael dy ddal.	You had been caught.
Roedd e wedi cael ei fwyta.	It had been eaten.

To say 'by' someone, use **gan**:

Mae'r bwyd wedi cael ei fwyta gan y bechgyn.
The food has been eaten by the boys.

2. Numbers – Ordinals:

1st	**cyntaf**
2nd	**ail**
3rd	**trydydd**
4th	**pedwerydd**
5th	**pumed**
6th	**chweched**
7th	**seithfed**
8th	**wythfed**
9th	**nawfed**
10th	**degfed**
100th	**canfed**

All except **cyntaf** are put before the noun:

y tîm cyntaf	the 1st team
y trydydd tîm	the 3rd team

Useful Words and Phrases

Days of the Week

dydd Llun	Monday	**nos Lun**	Monday night
dydd Mawrth	Tuesday	**nos Fawrth**	Tuesday night
dydd Mercher	Wednesday	**nos Fercher**	Wednsday night
dydd Iau	Thursday	**nos Iau**	Thursday night
dydd Gwener	Friday	**nos Wener**	Friday night
dydd Sadwrn	Saturday	**nos Sadwrn**	Saturday night
dydd Sul	Sunday	**nos Sul**	Sunday night

Times of Day

heddiw	today
yfory	tomorrow
ddoe	yesterday
bore ma	this morning
prynhawn ma	this afternoon
heno	tonight
bore yfory	tomorrow morning
bore ddoe	yesterday morning
neithiwr	last night
nos yfory	tomorrow night

Months of the Year

Ionawr	January
Chwefror	February
Mawrth	March
Ebrill	April
Mai	May
Mehefin	June

Gorffennaf	July
Awst	August
Medi	September
Hydref	October
Tachwedd	November
Rhagfyr	December

ym mis Ionawr	in January
ym mis Chwefror	in February

SEASONS

gwanwyn	spring	**yn y gwanwyn**	in spring
haf	summer	**yn yr haf**	in summer
hydref	autumn	**yn yr hydref**	in autumn
gaeaf	winter	**yn y gaeaf**	in winter

TIME

un o'r gloch	1 o'clock
dau o'r gloch	2 o'clock
tri o'r gloch	3 o'clock
pedwar o'r gloch	4 o'clock
pump o'r gloch	5 o'clock
chwech o'r gloch	6 o'clock
saith o'r gloch	7 o'clock
wyth o'r gloch	8 o'clock
naw o'r gloch	9 o'clock
deg o'r gloch	10 o'clock
un ar ddeg o'r gloch	11 o'clock
deuddeg o'r gloch	12 o'clock

chwarter i	a quarter to (followed by soft mutation)
chwarter wedi	a quarter past
hanner awr wedi	half past
pum munud wedi	5 past
pum munud i	5 to (followed by soft mutation)
deg munud wedi	10 past
deg munud i	10 to (followed by soft mutation)
ugain munud wedi	20 past
ugain munud i	20 to (followed by soft mutation)
pum munud ar hugain wedi	25 past
pum munud ar hugain i	25 to (followed by soft mutation)

FESTIVALS

Dydd Calan	New Year's Day
Dydd Gŵyl Dewi	St. David's Day (March 1st)
y Pasg	Easter
Calan Mai	May 1st
y Sulgwyn	Whitsun (7th Sunday after Easter)
Dydd Glyndŵr	Owain Glyndŵr's Day (Sept. 16)
Calan gaeaf	Halloween
y Nadolig	Christmas
Dydd San Steffan	Boxing Day

COUNTRIES

yr Almaen	Germany	**Gwlad Belg**	Belgium
yr Alban	Scotland	**Lloegr**	England
America	America	**Llydaw**	Brittany
Ariannin	Argentina	**Norwy**	Norway
Awstralia	Australia	**Rwsia**	Russia
Awstria	Austria	**Sbaen**	Spain
Cymru	Wales	**y Swistir**	Switzerland
Ffrainc	France	**yr Eidal**	Italy
Groeg	Greece		

Useful Phrases

Welsh – English

Beth yw ... yn Gymraeg?	What is ... in Welsh?
Beth yw pris y ...?	What's the price of ... ?
Ble?	Where?
Ble mae ...?	Where is ... ?
Pryd?	When?
Faint?	How much?
Bore da.	Good morning.
Croeso.	Welcome.
Dewch i mewn.	Come in.
Diolch yn fawr.	Thank you very much.
Dyma ...	This is ...
Eisteddwch.	Sit down.
Esgusodwch fi.	Excuse me.
Faint yw ...?	How much is ...?
Falch i gwrdd â chi.	Pleased to meet you.
Ga i ...?	May I ...? May I have ...?
Ga i helpu?	May I help?
Hwyl, Hwyl fawr.	Good-bye.
Iechyd da!	Cheers! (Good health!)
i'r chwith	to the left
i'r dde	to the right
Mae hi'n braf.	It's fine.
Nos da.	Good night.
Noswaith dda.	Good evening.
Oes ... 'da chi?	Have you got ...?
Os gwelwch yn dda.	Please.
Prynhawn da.	Good afternoon.
Shwmae? / Sut da'ch chi?	How are you?
Siaradwch yn araf.	Speak slowly.
Unwaith eto.	Once again.
Wi'n dysgu Cymraeg.	I'm learning Welsh.
yn dda iawn	very well
yn syth ymlaen	straight ahead

English – Welsh

Cheers! (Good health!)	**Iechyd da!**
Come in.	**Dewch i mewn.**
Excuse me.	**Esgusodwch fi.**
Good afternoon.	**Prynhawn da.**
Good-bye.	**Hwyl, Hwyl fawr.**
Good evening.	**Noswaith dda.**
Good morning.	**Bore da.**
Good night.	**Nos da.**
How are you?	**Shwmae? / Sut da'ch chi?**
Have you got ...?	**Oes ... 'da chi?**
Where?	**Ble?**
When?	**Pryd?**
How much?	**Faint?**
How much is ...?	**Faint yw ...?**
I'm learning Welsh.	**Wi'n dysgu Cymraeg.**
It's fine.	**Mae hi'n braf.**
May I ...? / May I have ...?	**Ga i ...?**
May I help?	**Ga i helpu?**
Once again.	**Unwaith eto.**
Please.	**Os gwelwch yn dda.**
Pleased to meet you.	**Falch i gwrdd â chi.**
Sit down.	**Eisteddwch.**
Speak slowly.	**Siaradwch yn araf.**
straight ahead.	**yn syth ymlaen.**
Thank you very much.	**Diolch yn fawr.**
This is ...	**Dyma ...**
to the left	**i'r chwith**
to the right	**i'r dde**
very well	**yn dda iawn**
Welcome.	**Croeso.**
What's the price of ...?	**Beth yw pris y ...?**
What is ... in Welsh?	**Beth yw ... yn Gymraeg?**
Where is ...?	**Ble mae ...?**

Key to the Exercises

LESSON 1

4. Examples:
    Ydych chi'n siarad Cymraeg?
    Ydych chi'n siarad Ffrangeg?
    Ydych chi'n siarad Saesneg?
    Ydych chi'n siarad Eidaleg?

5. Examples:
    Ydw, tipyn bach
    Na

6. Examples:
    Rwy'n siarad Almaeneg.
    Rwy'n siarad Eidaleg.
    Rwy'n deall Cymraeg.
    Rwy'n siarad Saesneg.

LESSON 2

4. Examples:
    Mae hi'n bwrw glaw heno.
    Bydd hi'n sych yfory.
    Mae hi'n sych heddiw.
    Bydd hi'n oer yfory.
    Mae hi'n braf bore ma.

5. Examples:
    Ydy hi'n bwrw glaw heddiw?
    Ydy hi'n braf heddiw?
    Fydd hi'n braf yfory?
    Fydd hi'n sych yfory?

Lesson 3

4. Examples:
Pryd mae'r trên yn cyrraedd?
Pryd mae'r trên yn mynd?
Pryd mae'r bws yn gadael?

5. b) Mae'r trên yn gadael Bangor am saith o'r gloch.
c) Mae'r bws yn gadael Caerdydd am un o'r gloch.
d) Mae'r bws yn gadael Llanelli am chwech o'r gloch.
e) Mae'r trên yn mynd i Abertawe am naw o'r gloch.

Lesson 4

4. Examples:
Rydw i'n hoffi nofio yn y môr.
Rydw i'n hoffi gweld ffilmiau yn y sinema.
Mae hi'n hoffi gweithio yn y llyfrgell.
Rydyn ni'n hoffi dysgu Cymraeg yn America.
Maen nhw'n hoffi byw yn Abertawe.

5. Examples:
Athrawes ydw i.
Clerc ydw i.
Gwraig tŷ ydw i.

Lesson 5

4. Examples:
Ydych chi'n gwybod ble mae'r llyfrgell?
Ydych chi'n gwybod ble mae'r sinema?
Ydy'r tacsi'n mynd i'r gwesty?
Ydy'r tacsi'n mynd i'r theatr?

5. Examples:
   Ydw; Ydw; Ydy; Ydy

6. **Ewch i'r chwith.**
   Ewch i'r dde.
   Ewch yn syth ymlaen.
   Ewch i'r stryd fawr.
   Ewch i'r sinema.
   Ewch i'r llyfrgell.
   Ewch i'r gwesty.

7. Examples:
   Ewch yn syth ymlaen i'r gwesty. Ewch i'r chwith i'r llyfrgell.
   Ewch yn syth ymlaen i'r sinema. Ewch i'r dde i'r stryd fawr.

LESSON 6

1. Examples:
   Dw i ddim yn hoffi ffilmiau.
   Dw i ddim yn hoffi dramâu.
   Dyw hi ddim yn hoffi nofelau.

2. I like the novel, but I don't like the film.
   I like walking, but I don't like swimming.
   I like coffee, but I don't like tea.
   I like Beethoven, but I don't like Mozart.

3. **Rwy'n hoffi Schubert, ond dw i ddim yn hoffi Brahms.**
   Rwy'n hoffi nofelau, ond dw i ddim yn hoffi dramâu.
   Rwy'n hoffi Vermont, ond dw i ddim yn hoffi Abertawe.
   Rwy'n hoffi ffilmiau James Bond, ond dw i ddim yn hoffi
   ffilmiau Spielberg.
   Rwy'n hoffi dal bws, ond dw i ddim yn hoffi cerdded.

Lesson 7

1. Mae car 'da fi.
    Mae llety 'da fi.
    Mae ystafell sengl 'da fi.
    Mae gwely dwbl 'da fi.
    Mae lle parcio 'da fi.

2. Examples:
    a) Oes, mae car 'da fi.
    b) Na, does dim cawod 'da fi yn yr ystafell wely.
    c) Oes, mae gwely dwbl 'da fi.
    d) Na, does dim gwely sengl 'da fi.

3. Rwy'n chwilio am ystafell sengl.
    Am sawl noson?
    Am un noson.
    Ga i ystafell ddwbl?
    Oes tŷ bach 'da hi.
    Oes, a chawod.
    Ga i'r ystafell, os gwelwch yn dda?

Lesson 8

1. Ga i wydraid o win, os gwelwch yn dda?
    Ga i hanner peint o gwrw, os gwelwch yn dda?
    Ga i botel o ddŵr, os gwelwch yn dda?
    Ga i beint o seidir, os gwelwch yn dda?
    Ga i wydraid o win gwyn, os gwelwch yn dda?
    Rwy'n moyn sudd afal, os gwelwch yn dda.
    Rwy'n moyn sudd oren, os gwelwch yn dda.
    Rwy'n moyn gwydraid o win coch, os gwelwch yn dda.
    Rwy'n moyn hanner peint o Guinness, os gwelwch yn dda.

2. pum punt; dwy bunt pum deg; tair punt pum deg; saith punt;
    deg punt; un bunt pum deg; wyth punt; naw punt

LESSON 9

1. Beth sy i frecwast?
   Ga i gwpaned o goffi du?
   Rwy'n moyn bara brown, os gwelwch yn dda.
   Oes llaeth 'da chi?
   Ga i gig moch, tost ac wy?

2. gwin gwyn; brecwast twym; bara brown; plât glân

3. llwy lân; ffilm dda; fforc frwnt

LESSON 10

1. Examples:
   Rwy wedi bwyta tost i frecwast.
   Mai hi wedi yfed te i frecwast.
   Rwy wedi bwyta sglodion i ginio.

2. Examples:
   I frecwast, rwy wedi bwyta wy a chig moch. Rwy wedi yfed te.
   I ginio, rwy wedi bwyta cyw a thatws. Rwy wedi yfed coffi.

LESSON 11

1. Rwy'n prynu llyfrau, casetiau a recordiau.
   Mae hi wedi prynu tapiau, sgertiau a sgarffiau i'r merched.
   Maen nhw wedi prynu trowsusau i'r bechgyn.

2. pum punt yr un; dwy bunt y pwys; deg punt y pâr

3. Rwy wedi bod yn siopa'r bore ma. Rwy wedi mynd i'r siop
   ddillad a'r siop lyfrau. Rwy wedi prynu siaced, pum llyfr
   a thâp.

Lesson 12

1. Examples:
    Mae'n rhaid i fi brynu stampiau.
    Mae'n well i chi ffonio i America.
    Mae'n bryd iddo fe anfon llythyr.
    Mae'n hen bryd i chi ffonio'r plant.

2. a) **Mae angen pum stamp pedwar deg tair ceiniog arna i.**
    b) **Rwy eisiau ffonio i America.**
    c) **Faint yw'r cerdyn ffôn?**
    d) **Ble galla i bostio llythyrau?**
    e) **Rwy'n chwilio am swyddfa'r post.**

Lesson 13

1. Examples:
    Ro'n i'n gyrru yn y car i Fangor.
    Ro'n i'n mynd yn y trên i Aberystwyth.
    Ro'n i'n rhedeg ar yr heol i'r Bala.

2. Examples:
    Ro'n i yn yr Almaen.
    Ro'n i yn Ewrop.
    Ro'n i yn yr Unol Daleithiau.

Lesson 14

1. **fy nhad; fy mhentref; fy nhref; fy ninas; fy ngwlad;**
    fy ngwely; fy mhabell; fy nghar; fy masged

2. Examples:
    Mae fy nghath yn dost.
    Mae fy nghi yn cysgu.
    Roedd fy ngheffyl yn cadw sŵn.

Lesson 15

1. fy nghar i; fy ngwlad i; fy mhen i; fy nghoes i
   ei dŷ fe; ei ardd e; ei bapur e; ei fam e; ei dref e

2. Wi'n gwybod bod annwyd arna i.
   Wi'n gwybod fy mod i'n dost.
   Wi'n gwybod fy mod i'n dod.
   Wi'n gwybod fy mod i'n aros mewn gwesty.
   Wi'n gwybod ei fod e'n gallu talu.
   Wi'n gwybod bod yswiriant 'da hi.

3. Wi'n ei thalu hi.
   Mae'r meddyg yn ei gweld hi.
   Mae'r dyn yn cael cinio ac yn ei fwyta fe.
   Mae hi'n gofyn am wydraid o win ac yn ei yfed e i gyd.

Lesson 16

1. Examples:
   Gweles i Huw yn chwarae yn y gêm.
   Gweles i Abertawe yn colli'r gêm.
   Gweles i Gaerdydd yn ennill y gêm.

2. Gweles i'r meddyg; Sgories i gôl; Prynes i docyn;
   Es i i'r gêm; Enilles i'r gêm; Colles i'r tocyn

Lesson 17

1. Examples:
   Mae'r bwyd wedi cael ei fwyta.
   Mae'r gwin wedi cael ei yfed.
   Mae'r tocyn wedi cael ei brynu.
   Mae'r bag wedi cael ei ffeindio.

2. a) **Mae'r bara wedi cael ei fwyta.**
    b) **Mae'r llyfr wedi cael ei ddarllen.**
    c) **Mae'r ffilm wedi cael ei gweld.**
    d) **Mae'r bag wedi cael ei golli.**

Dictionary

CYMRAEG – SAESNEG
WELSH – ENGLISH

When looking for a Welsh word in a dictionary, remember that the first letter of Welsh words can change, because of the various forms of mutation.

Words which seem to begin with a vowel (a, e, i, o, u, w, y) may really start with **g**.

These changes can occur:

Soft mutation

c	>	g	p	>	b	t	>	d
g	>	/	b	>	f	d	>	dd
ll	>	l	m	>	f	rh	>	r

Nasal mutation

c	>	ngh	p	>	mh	t	>	nh
g	>	ng	b	>	m	d	>	n

Aspirate mutation

c	>	ch	p	>	ph	t	>	th

Here is the Welsh alphabet:

A, B, C, CH, D, DD, E, F, FF, G, NG, H, I, J, L, LL, M, N, O, P, PH, R, RH, S, T, TH, U, W, Y.

Because of the combination letters which denote one sound, **ng**, for example, will be found before **g** and not after **n**.

These abbreviations are used:

(a)	adjective
(adv)	adverb
(f)	feminine noun
(c)	conjunction
(m)	masculine noun
(p)	pronoun
(pl)	plural
(pr)	preposition
(v)	verb

The plural of a noun is shown after /.

A

a (c) and
â (pr) with
Abertawe Swansea
Aberteifi Cardigan
ac (c) and
achau (pl) family tree
aderyn /adar (m) bird
afal /-au (m/f) apple
afon /-ydd (f) river
yr Alban (f) Scotland
allwedd /-i (f) key
yr Almaen (f) Germany
Almaeneg (f) German
am (pr) for, at
America (f) America
Americanes /–au American (f)
Americanwr/Americanwyr
    American (m)
angladd /-au (m) funeral
anifail /anifeiliaid (m) animal
annwyd (m) cold
annwyl (a) dear
anrheg /-ion (f) present
ar (pr) on
ar ddihun (adv) awake

ar goll (adv) lost
ar hyd (pr) along
araf (a) slow
arall (a) other
arddangosfa/arddangosfeydd (f)
    exhibition
arian (a) silver, (m) money
aros (v) wait
aros am (v) wait for
arwydd /-ion (f/m) sign
athrawes /-au (f) teacher
athro /athrawon (m) teacher
aur (a) gold
awyr (f) air
awyren /-nau (f) airplane

B

baban /-od (m) baby
bach (a) small, little
bachgen /bechgyn (m) boy
bag /-iau (m) bag
bag llaw (m) handbag
bai /beiau (m) fault
banana /-s (m) banana
banc /-iau (m) bank

bar /-rau (m) bar
bara (m) bread
basged /-i (f) basket
beic /-iau (m) bicycle
berwi (v) boil
beth? what?
bil /-iau (m) bill
bisgïen / bisgedi (f) biscuit
blasus (a) tasty
ble? where?
ble mae? where is?
blodyn /blodau (m) flower
blows /-ys (f) blouse
blwyddyn/blynyddoedd (f) year
blynedd (pl) years
bod (pr) that, (v) be
bore /-au (m) morning
bowlen /-ni (f) bowl
braf (a) fine
braich /breichiau (f) arm
brawd /brodyr (m) brother
brecwast /-au (m) breakfast
brest (f) chest
bresychen /bresych (f) cabbage
brithyll /-od (m) trout
bronglwm (m) bra
brown (a) brown
brwnt (a) dirty
brwsh /-ys (m) brush
bryn /-iau (m) hill
buwch /buchod (f) cow
bwrdd /byrddau (m) table
bwrw eira (v) snow
bwrw glaw (v) rain
bws /bysus (m) bus
bwyd /-ydd (m) food
bwydlen /-ni (f) menu
bwyta (v) eat
byd (m) world
bydd (v) will
bys /-edd (m) finger

C

cadair /cadeiriau (f) chair
cadw (v) keep
cadw sŵn (v) make a noise
cae /-au (m) field
cael (v) have
Caer Chester
Caerdydd Cardiff
Caerfyrddin Carmarthen
caffe /-s (m) café
calendr /-au (m) calendar
calon /-au (f) heart
camera/camerâu (m) camera
cân /caneuon (f) song
canol (m) center
canolfan hamdden (f) leisure
    center
cant hundred
canwr /cantorion (m) singer
car /ceir (m) car
cariad/-on (m) love, sweetheart
carped /-i (m) carpet
caru (v) love
casét /casetiau (m) cassette
cath /-od (f) cat
cawod /-ydd (f) shower
caws (m) cheese
ceffyl /-au (m) horse
cefn /-au (m) back
cefnder /-oedd (m) cousin
ceg /-au (f) mouth
cenedl /cenhedloedd (f) nation
cerdded (v) walk
cerddorfa/cerddorfeydd (f)
    orchestra
cerdyn /cardiau (m) card
cês /cesys (m) case
ci /cŵn (m) dog
cic /-iau (f) kick
cic gosb (f) penalty, free kick
cic rydd (f) free kick

cig /-oedd (m) meat
cig moch (m) bacon
cinio /ciniawau (m/f) lunch, dinner
clawdd /cloddiau (m) hedge
clerc /-od (m) clerk
clir (a) clear
cloc /-iau (m) clock
clust /-iau (f) ear
coch (a) red
codi (v) get up, raise, pick up
coeden /coed (f) tree
coes /-au (f) leg
coffi (m) coffee
cofion gorau fond regards
coleg /-au (m) college
colli (v) lose
côr /corau (m) choir
coridor /-au (m) corridor
cost /-au (f) cost
crap (f) smattering
creision (pl) crisps, chips
croeso (m) welcome
crys /-au (m) shirt
cul (a) narrow
cwmni (m) company
cŵn (pl) dogs
cwpan /-au (m/f) cup
cwpaned (m) cupful
cwrdd â (v) meet
cwrw (m) beer
cwstard (m) custard
cwyno (v) complain
cyfanswm (m) total
cyfeiriad /-au (m) address
cyfenw /-au (m) surname
cyfnither /-oeddd (f) cousin
cylchfan /-nau (f) roundabout,
    traffic circle
cyllell /cyllyll (f) knife
cymdeithasol (a) social
Cymraeg (f) Welsh
Cymraes (f) Welshwoman

Cymreig (a) Welsh
Cymro /Cymry (m) Welshman
Cymru (f) Wales
cymryd (v) take
cymylog (a) cloudy
cyngerdd/cyngherddau (f/m)
    concert
cynnwys (v) include
cyntaf (a) first
cyrraedd (v) arrive
cyw /-ion (m) chicken

CH
chi (p) you
chithau (p) you (too)
chwaer /chwiorydd (f) sister
chwaith (adv) either
chwarae (v) play
chwaraewr /chwaraewyr (m)
    player
chwe /chwech six
chwilio (v) look for, search
chwith left

D
da (a) good
dafad /defaid (f) sheep
dal (v) catch
dan (pr) under
dant /dannedd (m) tooth
darlithydd /darlithwyr (m)
    lecturer
darllen (v) read
darlun /-iau (m) picture
daro! dear!
dau two
de (m) south
deall (v) understand
dechrau (v) start
deffro (v) wake up
deg ten
dere! come!

desg /-iau (f) desk
dewch (v) come
dewis (v) choose
dewis /-iadau (m) choice
dillad (pl) clothes
dim (m) nothing
dim aros no waiting
dinas /-oedd (f) city
Dinbych Denbigh
diod /-ydd (f) drink
diolch (m) thanks
diolch byth thank goodness
disg /-iau (m) disk
di-waith (a) unemployed
diwedd (m) end
diwethaf (a) last
dod (v) come
dosbarth /-iadau (m) class
drama /dramâu (f) drama
dros (pr) over
drud (a) expensive
du (a) black
dwbl (a) double
dŵr (m) water
dwy two
dwyn (v) steal
dychwel (v) return
dydd /-iau (m) day
dyma here is, here are
dyn /-ion (m) man
dysgu (v) learn, teach

DD
dde (adv) right
ddoe (adv) yesterday

E
edrych (v) look
eglwys /-i (f) church
ei (p) her, his
eich (p) your
Eidaleg (f) Italian

eidion (m) beef
ein (p) our
eirin gwlanog (pl) peaches
eirinen /eirin (f) plum
eisiau (m, v) want
eistedd (v) sit
eliffant /-od (m) elephant
ennill (v) win
enw /-au (m) name
enw cyntaf (m) first name
eog /-iaid (m) salmon
er mwyn popeth for goodness'
  sake
ers (pr) since, for
esgid /-iau (f) shoe
esusodwch fi excuse me
eto (adv) again, yet
eu (p) their

F
fan'na (adv) over there
fe [confirms the verb]
fi (p) me
fy (p) my
fydd (c) will?

FF
ffatri /ffatrioedd (f) factory
ffeindio (v) find
ffenestr /-i (f) window
fferm /-ydd (f) farm
ffermwr /ffermwyr (m) farmer
ffilm /-iau (f) film
ffliw (m) flu
ffôn /ffonau (m) telephone
ffonio (v) phone
fforc /ffyrc (f) fork
ffordd /ffyrdd (f) way
ffordd fawr (f) main road
ffowlyn /ffowls (m) chicken
Ffrainc (f) France
Ffrangeg (f) French

ffresh (a) fresh
ffrio (v) fry
ffrog /-iau (f) frock
ffrwythau (pl) fruit
ffurflen /-ni (f) form

G
ga i (v) may I have
gadael (v) leave
gallu (v) be able to
galw (v) call
galwad /-au (f) call
galwyn /-i (m) gallon
gan (pr) by
gardd /gerddi (f) garden
garej /-ys (f) garage
gellygen /gellyg (f) pear
gêm /gemau (f) game
glas (a) blue
gofyn (v) ask
gogledd (m) north
gogoneddus (a) wonderful
gôl /-iau (f/m) goal
golau (a) light
golau /goleuadau (m) light
golff (m) golf
gormod (adv) too much
gorsaf /-oedd (f) station
gorsaf betrol (f) petrol station
gram /-au (m) gram
grawnwin (pl) grapes
gwaith (m) work
gwallt (pl) hair
gwasanaethau (pl) services
gwefus /-au (f) lip
gweithio (v) work
gweithiwr /gweithwyr (m) worker
gweld (v) see
gwell (a) better
gwely /-au (m) bed
gwersyll /-oedd (m) camp
gwersylla (v) camp

gwerth (m) value
gwerthu (v) sell
gwesty /gwestai (m) hotel
gwin /-oedd (m) wine
gwlad /gwledydd (f) country
gwlân (m) wool
gwneud (v) do, make
gwraig tŷ /gwragedd tŷ (f) housewife
gwres (m) fever
gwybod (v) know
gwybodaeth (f) information
gwydraid (m) glassful
gwyliau (pl) holidays
gwyn (a) white
gwyrdd (a) green
gyda (pr) with
gyrru (v) drive
gyrrwr /gyrwyr (m) driver

H
halen (m) salt
ham (m) ham
hanner /haneri (m) half
hapus (a) happy
haul /heuliau (m) sun
hawdd (a) easy
haws (a) easier
heb (pr) without
heddiw (adv) today
heddlu /-oedd (m) police force
heddwch (m) peace
helo hello
hen (a) old
hen ddigon enough by far
heno (adv) tonight
heol /-ydd (f) road
heulog (a) sunny
hi (p) she, her
hir (a) long
hoff (a) fond, favorite
hoffi (v) like

hosan /sanau (f) sock, stocking
hufen iâ (m) ice cream
hwn (p, a) this
hwyl good-bye
hwyl fawr good-bye
hy (a) bold
hyd (pr) until
hyfryd (a) pleasant, lovely
hyn (p,a) this, these
hynt (f) story, journey

I

i (pr) to
i gyd (adv) all
iâ (m) ice
iâr /ieir (f) hen
iawn (a) very, fine
ie yes
iechyd da good health, cheers
inc /-iau (m) ink

J

jam /-iau (m) jam
jin (m) gin
jîns (m) jeans
jwg /jygiau (m) jug

L

lamp /-au (f) lamp
lemwn /-au (m) lemon
letys (m) lettuce
lifft /-iau (m) lift
lily /lilïau (f) lily
lôn /lonau (f) lane
lwc (f) luck

LL

llaeth (m) milk
llai (a) less, smaller
llaw /dwylo (f) hand
llawer (adv) a lot
llawn (a) full

lle /-fydd (m) place
lleden (f) plaice fish
lleidr /lladron (m) thief
lleol (a) local
llestri (pl) dishes
llety /lletyau (m) lodging
Lloegr (f) England
llogi (v) hire
llong /-au (f) ship
llwnc (m) throat
llwy /-au (f) spoon
llwyd (a) grey
llyfr /-au (m) book
llyfrgell /-oedd (f) library
llyfrgellydd /-ion (m) librarian
llygad /llygaid (m) eye
llyn /-noedd (m) lake
llysiau (pl) vegetables
llythyr /-au (m) letter (message)
llythyren /llythrennau (f) letter
  (of alphabet)

M

'ma (a) this
mae (v) there is, is
mam /-au (f) mother
mam-gu /mamau cu (f)
  grandmother
map /-iau (m) map
marmalêd (m) marmalade
mat /-iau (m) mat
mawr (a) big
meddyg /-on (m) doctor
meddygfa /meddygfeydd (f)
  doctor's office
mêl (m) honey
melyn (a) yellow
melys (a) sweet
menyn (m) cheese
menyw /-od (f) woman
merch /-ed (f) girl
mil thousand

min (m) edge
mis /-oedd (m) month
mlynedd (pl) [blynedd] years
mochyn /moch (m) pig
moddion (pl) medicine
Môn Anglesey
môr /moroedd (m) sea
moron (pl) carrots
moyn (v) want
munud /-au (m/f) minute
mwy (a) more, bigger
mwyaf (a) most, biggest
mwyn (a) mild, gentle
myfyriwr /myfyrwyr (m) student
mynd (v) go
mynydd /-oedd (m) mountain

N

na no
na (c) than
nabod (v) know
nain/neiniau (f) grandmother
nant /nentydd (m) brook
naw nine
nawfed (a) ninth
neu (c) or
neuadd /-au (f) hall
neuadd y dref (f) town hall
newid (m, v) change
newydd (a) new
newyddion (pl) news
nhw (p) they, them
ni (p) we, us
nicyrs (m) knickers
nodyn /nodiadau (m) note
nofel /-au (f) novel
nofio (v) swim
nonsens (m) nonsense
nos /-au (f) night
noson (f) night
noswaith /nosweithiau (f) evening
nyrs /-ys (f) nurse

O

o gwmpas (pr) around
oedolyn /oedolion (m) adult
oen /wyn (m) lamb
oer (a) cold
oes (v) is there?, yes
olew (m) oil
oren (a) orange
oren /-nau (m) orange

P

pa which
pabell /pebyll (f) tent
pac /-iau (m) pack
pacio (v) pack
palas /-au (m) palace
papur /-au (m) paper
papur tŷbach (m) toilet paper
pâr /parau (m) pair
parc /-iau (m) park
parcio (v) park
parsel /-i (m) parcel
pas /-ys (f) pass
pedwar four
peint /-iau (m) pint
peiriant /peiriannau (m) machine,
    engine
pêl-droed (f) football, soccer
pêl-fas (f) baseball
pell (a) far
pen tost (m) headache
pensiynwr /pensiynwyr (m)
    pensioner
pentref /-i (m) village
penwythnos /-au (m) weekend
perfformio (v) perform
persawr (m) perfume
pert (a) pretty
peth /-au (m) thing
petrol (m) petrol, gasoline
pin /-nau (m) pin
pinc (a) pink

plant (pl) children
plât /platiau (m) plate
platfform /-au (m) platform
plentyn /plant (m) child
plismon /plismyn (m) policeman
pob every
poeni (v) worry
popeth (m) everything
porc (m) pork
porffor (a) purple
post post
postio (v) post
pot /-iau (m) pot
potel /-i (f) bottle
prifysgol /-ion (f) university
pris /-iau (m) price
problem /-au (f) problem
pryd (m) time
pryd? when?
prydferth (a) beautiful
prynhawn /-au (m) afternoon
prynu (v) buy
pum /pump five
punt /punnoedd (f) pound (£)
pupur (m) pepper
pur (a) pure
pwdin /-au (m) pudding, sweet,
    dessert
pwll/pyllau (m) pit
pwll nofio (m) swimming pool
pwys /-au (m) pound (lb)
pwys o a pound of
pwysedd (m) pressure
pwyso (v) weigh
pys (pl) peas
pysgodyn /pysgod (m) fish

R
'r the
radio (m) radio
râs /rasys race
record /-iau (f) record

reis (m) rice
rownd /-iau (f) round
rownd (pr) around
Rwsia (f) Russia
Rwsieg (f) Russian
rygbi (m) rugby

RH
rhad (a) cheap
rhaff /-au (f) rope
rhaid (m) must
rhedeg (v) run
rheolwr /rheolwyr (m) manager
rhif /-au (m) number
rholyn /rholiau (m) roll
rhostio (v) roast
rhy (a) too
rhyfel /-oedd (m) war

S
Saenseg (f) English
Saesnes /–au (f) Englishwoman
Sais /Saeson (m) Englishman
saith seven
salad /-au (m) salad
sanau (pl) socks, stockings
sawl how many
sawl (a) several
saws (m) sauce
Sbaen (f) Spain
Sbaeneg (f) Spanish
sŵn (m) noise
swyddfa /swyddfeydd (f) office
sebon /-au (m) soap
sedd /-au (f) seat
sedd flaen (f) front seat
sedd gefn (f) back seat
sefyll (v) stand
selsigen /selsig (f) sausages
sengl (a) single
seren /sêr (f) star
sewin (m) sewin (fish)

sgarff /-au (f) scarf
sgert /-iau (f) skirt
sglodion (pl) chips
sgorio (v) score
sgrîn /sgrinau (f) screen
shwmae how are you
siaced /-i (f) jacket
siarad (v) speak
siec /-iau (f) check
sieri (m) sherry
silff /-oedd (f) shelf
sinema /sinemâu (m/f) cinema
siocled /-i (m) chocolate
siop /-au (f) shop
siopwr /siopwyr (m) shopkeeper,
    shopper
Sir Fôn (f) Anglesey
siwgr (m) sugar
siŵr (a) sure
siwt /-iau (f) suit
soser /-i (f) saucer
stamp /-iau (m) stamp
stryd /-oedd (f) street
sudd /-oedd (m) juice
sur (a) sour
sut? how?
sut'dach chi? how are you?
swper /-au (m) supper
swydd /-i (f) job
swyddfa /swyddfeydd office
swyddfa'r post (f) post office
sych (a) dry
symffoni /symffonïau (m)
    symphony
syth (a) straight

T
tabled /-i (f) pill
tacsi /-s (m) taxi
tad /-au (m) father
tad-cu /tadau cu (m) grandfather
tafarn (f) pub

taflu (v) throw
tafod /-au (m) tongue
taid /teidiau (m) grandfather
tair three
talu (v) pay
tân /tanau (m) fire
tarten (f) tart, pie
tatws (pl) potatoes
te (m) tea
tebot /-au (m) teapot
technegydd /technegwyr
    technician
tei /-s (m) tie
teiar /-s (m) tire
teledu /setiau teledu (m) television
theatr /-au (f) theater
ti (p) you
tic /-iau (m) tick
ticio (v) tick
tipyn bach a little
tocyn /-nau (m) ticket
tomato /-s (m) tomato
ton /-nau (f) wave
tonic (m) tonic
torri (v) break
torri lawr (v) break down
tost (m) toast
traffig (m) traffic
traffordd /traffyrdd (f)
    motorway
traphont /-ydd (f) viaduct
tref /-i (f) town
trên /trenau (m) train
tri three
troed /traed (f) foot
trons /-au (m) underpants
trowsus /-au (m) trousers
trwm (a) heavy
trwy (pr) through
trwyn /-au (m) nose
trydanwr /trydanwyr (m)
    electrician

tun /-iau (m) tin
twym (a) warm, hot
tŷ /tai (m) house
tŷ bach (m) toilet
tŷ bwyta (m) restaurant
Tyddewi St. David's
tyn (a) tight
tywel /-ion (m) towel
tywydd (m) weather
tywyll (a) dark

U

un one
Unol Daleithiau America United
    States of America
unrhyw (a) any
unwaith (adv) once

W

wedi has, have, after
wedyn (adv) then, afterwards
winc (f) wink
wrth (pr) by, near
wrth gwrs of course
wy /-au (m) egg

wyth eight
wythnos /-au (f) week

Y

y the
ydw yes
ydych (v) are, do
yfed (v) drink
yfory (adv) tomorrow
yma (a) this
yma (adv) here
ymlaen (adv) ahead, on
yn [part of verb mae]
yn (pr) in
yr the
yr un (adv) each
ysbyty /ysbytai (m) hospital
ysgafn (a) light (in weight)
ysgol /-ion (f) school
ysgrifennu (v) write
ysgrifenyddes /-au (f) secretary
ystafell /-oedd (f) room
ystafell fwyta (f) dining room
ystafell wely (f) bedroom
ystafell ymolchi (f) bathroom
yswiriant (m) insurance

ENGLISH – WELSH
SAESNEG – CYMRAEG

A
able gallu (v), galluog (a)
address cyfeiriad (m)
adult oedolyn
after wedi
afternoon prynhawn
afterwards wedyn
again eto
ahead ymlaen
air awyr
airplane awyren
all i gyd
along ar hyd
America America
American Americanes (f),
   Americanwr (m)
and a, ac
Anglesey Môn
animal anifail
any unrhyw
apple afal
arm braich
around o gwmpas
arrive cyrraedd
ask gofyn
at i, at
awake ar ddihun

B
baby baban
back cefn (m)
back seat sedd gefn
bacon cig moch
bag bag
banana banana
bank banc

bar bar (m)
basket basged
bathroom ystafell ymolchi
beautiful prydferth
bed gwely
bedroom ystafell wely
beef cig eidion
beer cwrw
better gwell
bicycle beic
big mawr
bigger mwy
bill bil
bird aderyn
biscuit bisgïen
black du
blouse blows
blue glas
boil berwi
bold hy
book llyfr
bottle potel
bowl bowlen
boy bachgen
bra bronglwm
bread bara
break torri
break down torri lawr
breakfast brecwast
brook nant
brother brawd
brown brown
brush brwsh (m), brwsio (v)
bus bws
buy prynu
by wrth (near), gan

C

cabbage bresychen
café caffe
calendar calendr
call galw (v), galwad (f)
camera camera
camp gwersyll (m), gwersylla (v)
car car
card cerdyn
Cardiff Caerdydd
Cardigan Aberteifi
Carmarthen Caerfyrddin
carpet carped
carrots moron
case cês
cassette casét
cat cath
catch dal
chair cadair
change newid (m, v)
cheap rhad
cheers! iechyd da!
cheese caws
check siec
chest brest
Chester Caer
chicken cyw, ffowlyn
child plentyn
children plant
chips sglodion
chocolate siocled
choice dewis
choir côr
choose dewis
church eglwys
cinema sinema
city dinas
class dosbarth
clear clir (a), clirio (v)
clerk clerc
clock cloc
clothes dillad

cloudy cymylog
coffee coffi
cold oer (a), annwyd (m)
college coleg
come dod
come! dewch!, dere!
company cwmni
complain cwyno
concert cyngerdd
country gwlad
cousin cefnder (m), cyfnither (f)
cow buwch
crisps creision
cup cwpan
cupful cwpaned
custard cwstard

D

dark tywyll
day dydd
dear annwyl (a)
dear! daro!
Denbigh Dinbych
desk desg
dining room ystafell fwyta
dinner cinio
dirty brwnt (a)
dishes llestri
disk disg
do gwneud
doctor meddyg
dog ci
dogs cŵn
drama drama
drink yfed (v), diod (f)
drive gyrru (v)
driver gyrrwr
dry sych

E

each yr un
ear clust

easier haws
easy hawdd
eat bwyta
edge ymyl
egg wy
eight wyth
either chwaith
electrician trydanwr
elephant eliffant
end diwedd
engine peiriant
England Lloegr
English Saesneg
evening noson
every pob
everything popeth
excuse me esgusodwch fi
exhibition arddangosfa
expensive drud
eye llygad

F
factory ffatri
family tree achau
far pell
farm fferm
farmer ffermwr
father tad
fault bai
favorite hoff
fever gwres
field cae
film ffilm
fine braf (a)
fine iawn (all right)
finger bys
fire tân
first cyntaf
first name enw cyntaf
fish pysgodyn
flower blodyn

flu ffliw
fond hoff
food bwyd
foot troed
football pêl-droed
for am, i (to), ers (since)
for goodness' sake er mwyn
    popeth
fork fforc
form ffurflen
four pedwar (m), pedair (f)
French Ffrangeg
fresh ffresh
frock ffrog
front seat sedd flaen
fruit ffrwythau
fry ffrio
full llawn
funeral angladd

G
gallon galwyn
game gêm
garage garej, modurdy
garden gardd
gas station gorsaf betrol
gasoline petrol
gentle mwyn
German Almaeneg
Germany yr Almaen
get up codi
gin jin
girl merch
glassful gwydraid
go mynd
goal gôl
gold aur
golf golff
good da
good-bye hwyl, hwyl fawr
gram gram

grandfather tad-cu, taid
grandmother mam-gu, nain
grapes grawnwin
green gwyrdd
grey llwyd

H
hair gwallt
half hanner
hall neuadd
ham ham
hand llaw
handbag bag llaw
happy hapus
has wedi
have cael, wedi
he fe, e
headache pen tost
heart calon
heavy trwm
hedge clawdd
hello helo, shwmae
hen iâr
her hi, ei (**possession**)
here yma
here is, here are dyma
hill bryn
him fe, e
hire llogi
his ei
holidays gwyliau
honey mêl
horse ceffyl
hospital ysbyty
hot twym, poeth
hotel gwesty
house tŷ
housewife gwraig tŷ
how? sut?
how are you? shwd ych chi?,
    sut'dach chi?

how many? sawl?
hundred cant

I
ice iâ
ice cream hufen iâ
in yn
include cynnwys
information gwybodaeth
ink inc
insurance yswiriant
is there? oes?
Italian Eidaleg

J
jacket siaced
jam jam
jeans jîns
job swydd
journey taith
jug jwg
juice sudd

K
keep cadw
key allwedd
kick cic
knickers nicyrs
knife cyllell
know gwybod
know gwybod, nabod (**a person**)

L
lake llyn
lamb oen
lamp lamp
lane lôn
last diwethaf
learn dysgu
leave gadael
lecture darlithydd
left chwith

leg coes
leisure center canolfan hamdden
lemon lemwn
less llai
letter llythyr (message)
letter llythyren (of alphabet)
lettuce letys
librarian llyfrgellydd
library llyfrgell
lift lifft
light ysgafn (weight), golau (m)
like hoffi (v), fel (c)
lilly lili
lip gwefus
little bach
little, a tipyn bach
local lleol
lodging llety
long hir
look edrych
look for chwilio am
lose colli
lost ar goll
lot llawer
lovely hyfryd
luck lwc
lunch cinio

M
machine peiriant
main road ffordd fawr
make gwneud
make a noise cadw sŵn
man dyn
manager rheolwr
map map
marmalade marmalêd
mat mat
may I, may I have ga i
me fi
meat cig
medicine moddion

meet cwrdd â
menu bwydlen
mild mwyn
milk llaeth, llefrith
minute munud
money arian
month mis
more mwy
morning bore
mother mam
motorway traffordd
mountain mynydd
mouth ceg
must rhaid
my fy

N
name enw (m)
narrow cul
nation cenedl
near wrth (pr), agos (a)
new newydd
news newyddion
night nos, noson (evening)
nine naw
ninth nawfed
no na
noise sŵn
nonsense nonsens
north gogledd
nose trwyn
note nodyn (m)
nothing dim byd
novel nofel
number rhif
nurse nurse

O
of course wrth gwrs
office swyddfa
oil olew
old hen

on ar
once unwaith
one un
or neu
orange oren (a, m)
orchestra cerddorfa
other arall
our ein
over dros (pr)
over there fan'na

P

pack pac
pair pâr
palace palas
paper papur
parcel parsel
park parc (m), parcio (v)
pass pas (m), pasio (v)
pay talu
peace heddwch
peaches eirin gwlanog
pear gellygen
peas pys
penalty cosb, cic gosb
pensioner pensiynwr
pepper pupur
perform perfformio
petrol petrol
pick up codi
picture darlun, llun
pie tarten
pig mochyn
pill tabled
pin pin
pink pinc
pint peint
pit pwll
place lle
plaice fish lleden
plate plât

platform platfform
play chwarae (v), drama (f)
player chwaraewr
pleasant hyfryd
plum eirinen
police force heddlu
policeman plismon
pork porc
post post (m), postio (v)
post office swyddfa'r
pot pot
potatoes tatws
pound punt (£), pwys (lb)
present anrheg (f), presennol (a)
pressure pwysedd
pretty pert
price pris
problem problem
pub tafarn
pudding pwdin
pure pur
purple porffor

R

race râs
radio radio
rain glaw (m), bwrw glaw (v)
raise codi
read darllen
record record
red coch
restaurant bwyty
return dychwel
rice reis
right dde
river afon
road heol
roast rhostio
roll rholyn (m)
room ystafell
rope rhaff

round rownd
roundabout cylchfan
rugby rygbi
run rhedeg
Russia Rwsia
Russian Rwsieg (f)

S

salad salad
salmon eog
salt halen
sauce saws
saucer soser
sausages selsig
scarf sgarff
school ysgol
score sgôr
Scotland yr Alban
screen sgrîn
sea môr
search chwilio
seat sedd
secretary ysgrifenyddes (f)
see gweld
sell gwerthu
services gwasanaethau
seven saith
several sawl
sewin sewin (**fish**)
she hi
sheep dafad
shelf silff
sherry sieri
ship llong
shirt crys
shoe esgid
shop siop
shopkeeper siopwr
shower cawod
silver arian
since ers

singer canwr
single sengl
sister chwaer
sit eistedd
six chwe, chwech
skirt sgert
slow araf
small bach
smaller llai
snow eira (m), bwrw eira (v)
soap sebon
social cymdeithasol
sock hosan
socks sanau
song cân
sour sur
south de
Spanish Sbaeneg
speak siarad
spoon llwy
St. Davids Tyddewi
stamp stamp
stand sefyll (v)
star seren
start dechrau
station gorsaf
steal dwyn
stocking hosan
stockings sanau
story stori
straight syth
straight ahead yn syth ymlaen
street stryd
student myfyriwr
sugar siwgr
suit siwt (f)
sun haul
sunny heulog
supper swper
sure siŵr
surname cyfenw
Swansea Abertawe

sweet pwdin (m), melys (a)
sweetheart cariad (m,f)
swim nofio
swimming pool pwll nofio
symphony symffoni

T
table bwrdd
take mynd â, cymryd
tart tarten
tasty blasus
taxi tacsi
tea te
teach dysgu
teacher athrawes (f), athro (m)
teapot tebot
technician technegydd
telephone ffôn (m), ffonio (v)
television teledu
ten deg
tent pabell
than na
thank goodness diolch byth
thanks diolch
that bod (pr, v)
the y, yr, 'r
theater theatr
their eu
them nhw
then wedyn
there is, there are mae
these hyn
they nhw
thing peth
this 'ma
this hyn
thousand mil
three tri (m), tair (f)
throat llwnc
throw taflu
tick tic (m)
ticket tocyn

tie tei (m)
tight tyn
time amser
tire teiar
to i
toast tost (m)
today heddiw
toilet paper papur tŷ bach
tomato tomato
tomorrow yfory
tongue tafod
tonic tonic
tonight heno
too rhy (a), hefyd (adv)
too much gormod
tooth dant
total cyfanswm
towel tywel
town hall neuadd y dref
traffic traffig
train trên (m)
tree coeden
trousers trowsus
trout brithyll
two dau (m), dwy (f)

U
United States of America (U.S.A.)
    Unol Daleithiau America
    (U.D.A.)
under dan
underpants trôns
understand deall
unemployed di-waith
university prifysgol
until hyd
us ni

V
value gwerth
vegetables llysiau
very iawn

viaduct traphont
village pentref

W
wake up deffro
Wales Cymru
walk cerdded
want moyn, eisiau
war rhyfel
warm twym
water dŵr
wave ton (f), chwifio (v)
way ffordd
we ni
weather tywydd
week wythnos
weekend penwythnos
weigh pwyso
welcome croeso (m)
Welsh Cymraeg (f), Cymreig (a)
Welsh people Cymry
Welshman Cymro
Welshwoman Cymraes
what? beth?
when? pryd?
where? ble?

which pa
white gwyn
will bydd
will? fydd?
win ennill
window ffenestr
wine gwin
wink winc (f)
with â, gyda
without heb
woman menyw
wonderful gogoneddus
wool gwlân
work gwaith (m), gweithio (v)
worker gweithiwr
world byd
worry poeni

Y
year blwyddyn
yellow melyn
yes ie, oes, ydy, oedd, bydd
yesterday ddoe
yet eto
you chi, ti
your eich, dy

Beginner's Welsh
with 2 Audio CDs

CD Track List

Disc One

1. The Welsh Alphabet: The Consonants
2. The Vowels
3. Other Combinations
4. Words that sound similar to English and mean the same
5. Words that sound fairly similar to English and mean the same
6. Words that sound similar to English but have a different meaning
7. Personal Names
8. Place Names
9. Lesson 1 Dialogue 1
10. Lesson 1 Dialogue 1 for repetition
11. Lesson 1 Dialogue 2
12. Lesson 1 Dialogue 2 for repetition
13. Lesson 1 Phrases & Vocabulary
14. Lesson 1 Additional Vocabulary
15. Lesson 2 Dialogue 1
16. Lesson 2 Dialogue 1 for repetition
17. Lesson 2 Dialogue 2
18. Lesson 2 Dialogue 2 for repetition
19. Lesson 2 Radio weather report
20. Lesson 2 Radio weather report for repetition
21. Lesson 2 Phrases & Vocabulary
22. Lesson 2 Additional Vocabulary
23. Lesson 3 Dialogue 1
24. Lesson 3 Dialogue 1 for repetition
25. Lesson 3 Dialogue 2
26. Lesson 3 Dialogue 2 for repetition
27. Lesson 3 Phrases & Vocabulary
28. Lesson 3 Additional Vocabulary

Disc Two

11. Lesson 12 Phrases & Vocabulary
12. Lesson 12 Additional Vocabulary
13. Lesson 13 Dialogue
14. Lesson 13 Dialogue for repetition
15. Lesson 13 Phrases & Vocabulary
16. Lesson 13 Additional Vocabulary
17. Lesson 14 Dialogue
18. Lesson 14 Dialogue for repetition
19. Lesson 14 Phrases & Vocabulary
20. Lesson 14 Additional Vocabulary
21. Lesson 15 Dialogue
22. Lesson 15 Dialogue for repetition
23. Lesson 15 Phrases & Vocabulary
24. Lesson 15 Additional Vocabulary
25. Lesson 16 Dialogue
26. Lesson 16 Dialogue for repetition
27. Lesson 16 Phrases & Vocabulary
28. Lesson 16 Additional Vocabulary
29. Lesson 17 Dialogue
30. Lesson 17 Dialogue for repetition
31. Lesson 17 Phrases & Vocabulary
32. Lesson 17 Additional Vocabulary
33. Lesson 17 Ordinal Numbers
34. Days of the Week
35. Times of Day
36. Months of the Year
37. Seasons
38. Time
39. Festivals
40. Countries
41. Useful Phrases, Welsh–English
42. Useful Phrases, English–Welsh

Welsh Interest Titles from Hippocrene Books . . .

Welsh-English/English-Welsh Dictionary & Phrasebook
Heini Gruffudd

Wales is, with England, Scotland, and Northern Ireland, one of the four constituent parts of the United Kingdom. More than half a million Welsh residents speak the Welsh language. With over 6,000 entries of vocabulary and essential phrases, a pronunciation guide, a basic Welsh grammar, and travel tips and useful cultural information, this two-way language guide offers travelers, students, and businesspeople the basic tools for travel and daily life in Wales.

6,000 entries • 309 pages • 3¾ x 7½ x 0-7818-1070-1 • $12.95pb • (577)

Welsh-English/English-Welsh Standard Dictionary
H. Meurig Evans

This completely modern and comprehensive dictionary contains over 50,000 entries, a detailed introduction to the Welsh language, modern and technological terms, and thematic appendices listing proverbs, place names, personal names, animals, plants and more.

50,000 entries • 618 pages • 5¼ x 8½ • 0-7818-0136-2 • $24.95pb • (116)

Wales: An Illustrated History
Henry Weisser

Here is a balanced, unbiased account that traces the key forces and developments through all the centuries of Welsh history from Roman occupation to the diverse nature of contemporary Wales.

170 pages • 5 x 7 • 0-7818-1070-1 • $12.95pb • (418)

Traditional Food from Wales
Bobby Freeman

Welsh food and customs through the centuries. This book combines over 260 authentic proven recipes, such as traditional favorites like *Blackberry Bread Pudding, Welsh Salt Duck,* and *Trout with Bacon,* with cultural and social history.

332 pages • 6 x 8½ • 0-7818-0527-9 • $24.95hc • (638)

Other related titles of interest
from Hippocrene...

Irish-English/English-Irish Dictionary and Phrasebook
Davidovic Mladen

This 1,400-word dictionary indicates pronunciation in English spelling and will swiftly acquaint visitors with a basic key vocabulary. Phrases cover travel, sightseeing, shopping, and recreation, and notes are provided on grammar, pronunciation, and dialect.

71 pages • 3½ x 7• 0-8705-2110-1 • $9.95pb • (385)

Irish-English / English-Irish Practical Dictionary
Cló Ruraí

A fully up-to-date, comprehensive and clearly presented bilingual dictionary with over 20,000 words and an introduction to the use of Irish. The ideal reference for learners and speakers of Irish.

251 pages • 4 x 6 • 0-7818-0777-8 • $12.95pb • (39)

Beginner's Irish with Audio CD
Gabriel Rosenstock

Beginner's Irish offers basic Irish language instruction, presenting grammar, vocabulary, and common phrases in clear, concise lessons. Review questions and exercises accompany each lesson. Historical and cultural material gives insight into customs and everyday situations. It is an ideal companion for students, travelers, and businesspeople.

145 pages • 5½ x 8½ • 0-7818-1099-X • $19.95pb • (121)

Feasting Galore Irish Style: Recipes and Food Lore From the Emerald Isle
Maura Laverty

Hippocrene Books is pleased to bring this classic cookbook, which was originally published in 1952, back into print for today's readers. Author Maura Laverty, a leading Irish playwright, novelist and culinary writer, beckons readers through the door of the traditional Irish kitchen, to the heart of the family's life. Each of the eleven chapters begins with an engaging anecdote that puts the food into its context—whether it is prepared to celebrate an occasion, to welcome guests, or even to seduce! Complete with charming black and white illustrations.

144 pages • 5½ x 8½ • 0-7818-0869-3 • $14.95hc • (94)

Scottish Gaelic-English/English-Scottish Gaelic Dictionary
R.W. Renton & J.A. MacDonald

Scottish Gaelic is the language of a hearty, traditional people, over 75,000 strong. This dictionary provides the learner or traveler with a basic, modern vocabulary and the means to communicate in a quick fashion.

162 pages • 4 x 6 • 0-7818-0316-0 • $9.95pb • (285)